Current
CONTROVERSIES

The Global Food Crisis

Other Books in the Current Controversies Series

The Global Food Crisis

Uma Kukathas, Book Editor

GREENHAVEN PRESS
A part of Gale, Cengage Learning

Detroit • New York • San Francisco • New Haven, Conn • Waterville, Maine • London

Christine Nasso, *Publisher*
Elizabeth Des Chenes, *Managing Editor*

© 2009 Greenhaven Press, a part of Gale, Cengage Learning

Articles in Greenhaven Press anthologies are often edited for length to meet page require-ments. In addition, original titles of these works are changed to clearly present the main thesis and to explicitly indicate the author's opinion. Every effort is made to ensure that Greenhaven Press accurately reflects the original intent of the authors. Every effort has been made to trace the owners of copyrighted material.

Cover image copyright AFP/Getty Images.

LIBRARY OF CONGRESS CATALOGING-IN-PUBLICATION DATA

The global food crisis / Uma Kukathas, book editor.
p. cm. -- (Current controversies)
Includes bibliographical references and index.
ISBN 978-0-7377-4613-6 (hardcover)
ISBN 978-0-7377-4612-9 (pbk.)
1. Food supply--Juvenile literature. 2. Food industry and trade--Juvenile litera-ture. 3. International trade--Juvenile literature. 4. International finance--Juvenile literature. I. Kukathas, Uma.
HD9000.5.G5825 2009
363.8--dc22
2009012958

Printed in the United States of America
1 2 3 4 5 6 7 13 12 11 10 09

Contents

No: Global Market Capitalism Has Not Caused the World Food Crisis

Chapter 2: Is the Demand for Biofuels Fueling the Global Food Crisis?

Yes: The Demand for Biofuels Is Fueling the Global Food Crisis

Chapter 3: Can Biotechnology Solve the Global Food Crisis?

Chapter 4: How Can the World Solve the Current Food Crisis?

Foreword

By definition, controversies are "discussions of questions in which opposing opinions clash" (Webster's Twentieth Century Dictionary Unabridged). Few would deny that controversies are a pervasive part of the human condition and exist on virtually every level of human enterprise. Controversies transpire between individuals and among groups, within nations and between nations. Controversies supply the grist necessary for progress by providing challenges and challengers to the status quo. They also create atmospheres where strife and warfare can flourish. A world without controversies would be a peaceful world; but it also would be, by and large, static and prosaic.

The Series' Purpose

The purpose of the Current Controversies series is to explore many of the social, political, and economic controversies dominating the national and international scenes today. Titles selected for inclusion in the series are highly focused and specific. For example, from the larger category of criminal justice, Current Controversies deals with specific topics such as police brutality, gun control, white collar crime, and others. The debates in Current Controversies also are presented in a useful, timeless fashion. Articles and book excerpts included in each title are selected if they contribute valuable, long-range ideas to the overall debate. And wherever possible, current information is enhanced with historical documents and other relevant materials. Thus, while individual titles are current in focus, every effort is made to ensure that they will not become quickly outdated. Books in the Current Controversies series will remain important resources for librarians, teachers, and students for many years.

In addition to keeping the titles focused and specific, great care is taken in the editorial format of each book in the series. Book introductions and chapter prefaces are offered to provide background material for readers. Chapters are organized around several key questions that are answered with diverse opinions representing all points on the political spectrum. Materials in each chapter include opinions in which authors clearly disagree as well as alternative opinions in which authors may agree on a broader issue but disagree on the possible solutions. In this way, the content of each volume in Current Controversies mirrors the mosaic of opinions encountered in society. Readers will quickly realize that there are many viable answers to these complex issues. By questioning each author's conclusions, students and casual readers can begin to develop the critical thinking skills so important to evaluating opinionated material.

Current Controversies is also ideal for controlled research. Each anthology in the series is composed of primary sources taken from a wide gamut of informational categories including periodicals, newspapers, books, U.S. and foreign government documents, and the publications of private and public organizations. Readers will find factual support for reports, debates, and research papers covering all areas of important issues. In addition, an annotated table of contents, an index, a book and periodical bibliography, and a list of organizations to contact are included in each book to expedite further research.

Perhaps more than ever before in history, people are confronted with diverse and contradictory information. During the Persian Gulf War, for example, the public was not only treated to minute-to-minute coverage of the war, it was also inundated with critiques of the coverage and countless analyses of the factors motivating U.S. involvement. Being able to sort through the plethora of opinions accompanying today's major issues, and to draw one's own conclusions, can be a complicated and frustrating struggle. It is the editors' hope that Current Controversies will help readers with this struggle.

Introduction

> *"The response to the global food crisis has not been a unified one . . . and a lack of a singular vision has been an enormous stumbling block in finding a solution."*

In the late 1990s, the prices of food worldwide had reached historic lows. The so-called Asian "green" revolution, which saw large increases in grain yields with the use of pesticides and modern agricultural methods, combined with higher food production in developed countries, contributed to the actual prices of staple foods falling to their lowest levels since the 1950s. But in 2000, food prices began to rise. The climb became gradually steeper, and in late 2006 costs suddenly spiked. In 2007 and 2008, the cost of basic foodstuffs surged, creating a global crisis when millions saw their food budgets rise beyond their means.

In less than three years, world food prices doubled; between April 2007 and April 2008 alone they rose by 85 percent. By early 2008, wheat was twice what it had been a year earlier. Rice, the staple food for about 3 billion people, tripled in cost. These staggering prices triggered riots and demonstrations around the world. A 400 percent increase in the cost of tortillas caused tens of thousands of Mexicans to march in protest in early 2007. In West Bengal, India, protesters destroyed stores carrying government-subsidized food, accusing owners of selling the rations on the black market. Riots exploded in Senegal, Mauritania, and Burkina Faso over high grain prices. In early 2008, demonstrators in Haiti tried to storm the National Palace, and in April, English pig farmers staged a protest over the rising cost of wholesale grain to feed their livestock.

In less than a decade, the world went from a seeming abundance of food at low prices to a dire shortage, in which American middle-class families were struggling and many of the poor were essentially priced out of the market. What caused this dramatic shift? How did this crisis that has reached every corner of the globe take shape? While nobody disputes the seriousness of the crisis, and especially its impact on the poorest nations around the world, there is surprisingly little agreement among economists, activists, and political leaders as to the exact causes of the global food crisis—and, as a result, what to do about it. There is some consensus that high oil prices, population growth, urbanization, and weather conditions collided to create a "perfect storm" in which demand for food has outstripped supply. However, debates continue to rage over whether other factors, such as flawed trade policies, agricultural practices, changing dietary habits, increased demand for biofuels, commodity speculation, and the global capitalist system are the true culprits.

At the June 2008 world food summit in Rome, convened by the United Nation's Food and Agriculture Organization (FAO), it was clear how divided the world is on the causes of the crisis and the strategies needed to combat the problem. The head of the FAO, Jacques Diouf, called upon nations to pledge $30 billion in assistance to the world's 862 million people suffering from hunger and malnutrition. The FAO organizers pointed to World Bank estimates that this number of poorly nourished people could rise by more than 100 million if aid is not provided soon. But Diouf's calls were largely ignored. Further, his suggestions that biofuels—and corn ethanol subsidies to U.S. farmers in particular—are the major cause for escalating food prices were met with irritation by ethanol-producing countries. While studies show that demand for cereal grains has gone up by 60 percent because of biofuel production, U.S. agriculture secretary, Ed Schafer, insisted that number was grossly exaggerated and that biofuels accounted for only a two or three percent increase in demand for grains.

The claims made by some Westerners—including, most famously, former U.S. President George W. Bush in May of 2008—that rising prices are partially the result of an increased appetite for meat by growing middle classes in China and India, was also met with scorn by Chinese and Indian delegations. Chinese agriculture minister Zhengcai Sun pointed out that China is a net exporter of grain and thus could not be responsible for the surge in consumption. Other Indian commentators, including Vandana Shiva, had earlier expressed outrage at the notion that Americans, who constitute 5 percent of the earth's population but consume a third of its resources, could point their finger at Indians. Shiva has noted that despite the myth of India as an "economic miracle," in truth the majority of Indians eat less now than they did ten years ago. She says this is because so many have lost their lands and livelihoods as a result of trade policies that force India to buy grains from subsidized Western farmers.

Farming subsidies by wealthy countries have been a source of bitterness for many in the developing world, and activists have long claimed that they obliterate any real notion of "free trade," prevent small farmers from competing in the world market, and distort food prices—which has now culminated in a food crisis on a disastrous scale. However, European and American farmers have objected to losing their subsidies, which they say they cannot operate without and still maintain the required high standards.

Another source of contention for some environmentalists is the notion that biotechnology promoted by the West is the best means for Third World farmers to increase their yields and feed themselves. Many environmental activists responding to the Rome summit lamented the fact that the FAO promotes only agricultural development that enriches agribusiness at the expense of the world's poor. Others have echoed this concern that biotechnology, which is heavily promoted by corporations who stand to profit from its use, is not a solution to the global food crisis and that, indeed, the use of chemical farming has contributed to the degradation of farmland and thus is at the root of the problem. However, numerous other experts, including the Nobel Prize-winning agronomist Norman E. Borlaug, dismiss anti-technology critics, arguing that only with the use of chemicals and biotechnology can the world hope to feed its 6.3 billion residents.

At the Rome summit and beyond, the response to the global food crisis has not been a unified one. Nations and groups with conflicting agendas have seen the problem very differently, and a lack of a singular vision has been an enormous stumbling block in finding a solution. The world financial crisis, which has gripped the world's attention after late 2008, has overshadowed the issue of food security. Food prices began to fall in 2009, but this drop is likely temporary. The food crisis remains a critical issue and one that must be addressed because, as events have shown, it threatens to destabilize not only people's health on a massive scale but also the peace and security of countries in every corner of the globe.

CHAPTER 1

Has Global Market Capitalism Caused the World Food Crisis?

Chapter Preface

When global food prices began to soar in 2007 and 2008, many American consumers were left reeling—and puzzling as to how these changes could have come about so rapidly, without apparent warning. Prices had held steady for a long time, and while the costs of other goods had risen over the decades, food had always been within easy reach of the middle class.

Many economists blamed increasing global demand and a number of natural disasters—from drought in major food exporting nations such as Australia and Ukraine to flooding in parts of Africa and the American Midwest—which shrunk supplies while demand continued to expand. However, other economists, environmentalists, and community activists have seen the problem quite differently. While climate change has affected food supplies, they have argued, the crisis facing the world is not due to natural forces, or even the forces of supply and demand, but is the result of bad economic policies and a capitalist system that have benefited the richest in the world at the expense of the poor.

According to Jayati Ghosh, a Professor of Economics at Jawaharlal Nehru University, in New Delhi, India, the 2007–2008 food crisis is very much man-made. He faults what he sees as a market-oriented framework that has governed most economic policy-making over the past two decades. The lack of public investment in agriculture, the emphasis on open trade, and the market orientation, he says, have resulted in farmers shifting their practices to produce cash crops rather than food crops. Agriculture as a for-profit business rather than a means to put food on the table has also put them at the mercy of large seed companies and corporations selling chemical fertilizers.

Ghosh also cites the impact on food prices of speculation in commodities. Food security activists and even United Nations officials have also made the argument that speculative investors are to blame for global food woes. With stock markets and the property sector in the United States weakening, speculators turned to food as a "safe haven" in which to pour their money, driving up prices. Private equity companies seeking to profit from price swings on the international commodities markets bought futures in food stocks, and this, combined with increasing demand for food, led to skyrocketing prices.

Looking at the earnings of some of the world's largest agribusinesses during the crisis shows that some have clearly profited from the world's misfortunes. In early 2008, Cargill Corporation's net earnings soared by 86 percent. Archer Daniels Midland, one of the world's largest agricultural processors of soy, corn, and wheat, increased its net earnings in the first three months of 2008 from $363 million to $517 million. The Mosaic Company, which sells chemical fertilizers, reported a 12-fold growth in the early months of 2008 because of a fertilizer shortage.

Not everyone sees global capitalism as the villain of the story, however. Many free-market economists continue to see the market mechanisms as being the best hope of bringing the crisis to an end. They view the crisis as the result, not of market forces and lack of regulation, but of the interventions of governments—including providing farming subsidies and erecting trade barriers—that have distorted markets, reduced incentives for farmers, and made it impossible for everyone to compete equally and fairly in the global marketplace. Without these mechanisms in place, they argue, a truly free market system would see prosperity for far greater numbers and limit the type of disasters currently seen in the world food situation.

Neoliberal Economic Strategies Have Created the Food Crisis

Jayati Ghosh

Jayati Ghosh is a professor at the Centre for Economic Studies and Planning at Jawaharlal Nehru University, New Delhi, India.

This is not a sudden and unexpected crisis: the signs have been around for some time now. Even though international bureaucrats have been referring to the current problems in the world food situation as 'a silent tsunami', the truth is that this one could easily have been seen to be coming. Even so, its impact has been powerful and already quite devastating, as food shortages and rapidly rising prices of food have adversely affected billions of people, especially the poor in the developing world.

It is also very much a man-made crisis, resulting not so much from ineluctable forces of global supply and demand as from the market-oriented and liberalising policies adopted by choice or compulsion in almost all countries. These policies have either neglected agriculture or allowed shifts in global prices to determine both cropping patterns and the viability of farming, and also generated greater possibilities of speculative activity in food items. Cultivators in developing countries have been ravaged by the fearsome combination of exposure to import competition from highly subsidised agriculture in developed countries, removal of domestic protection of inputs and reduced access to institutional credit—to the point that even the global increase in agricultural prices after 2002 did not compensate sufficiently to alleviate the pervasive agrarian crisis in much of the developing world.

Jayati Ghosh, "The Global Food Crisis," *Third World Resurgence*, April 2008. Copyright © 2008 Third World Network. All rights reserved. Reproduced by permission.

Features of the Crisis

What are the symptoms of this crisis? The most immediately evident feature is the recent rise in food prices. Globally, the prices of many basic food commodities have not risen faster for more than three decades. In fact, even in recent years, food prices internationally had shown only a modest increase until early 2007. But since then they have zoomed, such that International Monetary Fund (IMF) data show a more-than-40% increase in world food prices over 2007, and even more rapid increases in the first three months of [2008]. The UN [United Nations] Food and Agriculture Organisation (FAO) food price index, which includes national prices as well as those in cross-border trade, suggests that the average index for 2007 was nearly 25% above the average for 2006. Apart from sugar, nearly every other food crop showed very significant increases in price in world trade over 2007. This trend has accelerated in the first few months of 2008.

The increase has been marked in essential food grains that are staples for most of the world's population. Global wheat prices increased by 77% in 2007 and rice prices increased by nearly 20%, which are some of the most rapid annual increases in the past half-century. Since the start of 2008, world rice prices have soared even more, increasing by nearly one-and-a-half times just in the first 100 days of the year. Wheat prices have been highly volatile in the current year, increasing by 25% in one day and then falling even more sharply in early April [2008], but are still well above the levels of most of last year. The price of corn—another major staple especially in Latin America—has more than doubled [from 2006 to 2008].

Across developing countries there is evidence of growing shortage of food in retail trade, even if not always in domestic production. Price rises for food grains have varied in intensity according to how well different governments have been able to manage the global impact and ensure domestic supply. And prices of other food items—ranging from meat and vegetables to edible oils—have also skyrocketed.

The impact of this has been felt most sharply in poor countries where most people tend to spend around half of their family budgets on food items. There have already been food riots in countries as far apart as Haiti, Guinea, Mauritania, Mexico, Morocco, Egypt, Senegal, Uzbekistan, Yemen, Bangladesh, Philippines and Indonesia. And many more countries are threatened by social unrest as rising food prices cause not merely dissatisfaction but the spread of hunger. In several countries in Asia, such as Pakistan and Thailand, troops have been deployed to guard food stocks and prevent seizure of grain from warehouses.

Even the institutions that have encouraged policies that have brought the situation to this pass have had to sit up and take notice. The World Bank President now estimates that such high food prices could cause more than 100 million people in low-income countries to be pushed back into deeper poverty.

The Role of Increased Demand

There are many explanations being offered for the recent increase in global food prices. It has been argued that this is essentially demand-led, the result of several years of rapid economic growth and rising incomes in some of the most populous nations (particularly China and India), hence the growing demand for food. It is pointed out that as per capita incomes rise, even though people may spend a lower percentage of their income on food, the absolute amount of demand still increases. And even when they consume less food grain directly because of a change in food consumption patterns, the indirect demand for grain still increases, often more than proportionately, because of more demand for animal products, since livestock also need to be fed and some like cattle require even more grain than humans. It is estimated that each kilo of beef requires seven kilos of grain to be produced.

However, the contribution of increasing global demand, while it has a role, should not be overplayed, especially in the case of China. In fact, a study by Germany's National Office for Agricultural Produce Prices rejected the claims that growing demand in China is the main reason for the current spike in world food prices and said that China's alleged influence on markets is often exaggerated. It noted that while over the past decade Chinese domestic consumption of milk and dairy products rose by more than five times, the bulk of this increase in demand was satisfied by a simultaneous expansion in Chinese production. Currently China meets more than 90% of its needs in wheat, maize and rice, and it is aiming for producing 95% of its estimated future demand for these items.

In certain products, China's involvement in global markets has played a role in affecting prices. In 2006 and part of 2007 Chinese pork production had collapsed because of animal disease, causing higher imports of both pork and corn feed for pigs to increase domestic pork supply. Similarly, 40% of world production of soyabean is currently imported by China, largely for use as animal feed. Chinese imports of other primary products such as cotton, vegetable oils, rubber, timber and animal skins have soared. But these are not responsible for higher world prices of wheat and rice.

In any case, it should be noted that this is not the first time that the world economy has witnessed increases in income of a significant portion of the population, and these previous phases were not accompanied by such sharp increases in food prices.

Rather than these simplistic explanations, therefore, it is likely that there are other forces at work. Five major aspects affecting supply conditions have been crucial in changing global market conditions for food crops.

High Oil Prices

First, there is the impact of high oil prices, which affect agricultural costs directly and indirectly in a variety of ways. This is because of the growing significance of energy as an input in the cultivation process itself as well as in transporting food. Changing cultivation technology has meant ever-growing reliance on chemical fertilisers whose production costs are directly affected by oil prices. Greater mechanisation of agriculture in the form of tractors, harvesters and threshers requires more oil to run these machines. The spread of irrigation, especially ground water exploitation, requires energy in the form of diesel or electricity to run pump sets.

In addition to diverting corn output into non-food use, [biofuel production] has also reduced acreage for other crops.

This rise in energy costs has had more of an impact than before because in most countries, especially in the developing world, governments have reduced protection and subsidies on agriculture. This means that high costs of energy directly translate into higher costs of cultivation, and therefore higher prices of output.

Biofuels' Side Effects

Second, there is the biofuel factor: the impact of both oil prices and government policies in the US, Europe, Brazil and elsewhere that have promoted biofuels as an alternative to petroleum. This has led to significant shifts in acreage to the cultivation of crops that can produce biofuels, and diversion of such output to fuel production. For example, in 2006 the US diverted more than 20% of its maize production to the production of ethanol, Brazil used half of its sugarcane production to make biofuel, and the European Union used the greater part of its vegetable oil seeds production as well as imported vegetable oils to make biofuel.

The US has led this shift globally. President George Bush provided an impetus to domestic ethanol production by providing large subsidies, in a desperate attempt to reduce dependence upon petroleum once it became evident that the imperialist attempt to control Middle East oil supplies had come unstuck with the failed invasion of Iraq. According to the IMF, corn ethanol production in the United States has accounted for a minimum of 50% of the increase in global corn output since 2006.

In addition to diverting corn output into non-food use, this has also reduced acreage for other crops and has naturally reduced the available land for producing food. Soyabean production has been affected by the acreage shift, and therefore oilseed prices have gone up. Meanwhile, the use of maize to make ethanol has caused corn prices to rise, and increased the price of animal feed, thereby causing increased prices of livestock and therefore meat and dairy products.

The irony is that biofuels do not even fulfil the promises of ensuring energy security or retarding the pace of global warming. Ethanol production is extremely energy-intensive, so it does not really lead to any energy saving. Even in countries like Brazil where sugarcane rather than corn is used to produce ethanol, it has been argued that the push for such production has led to large-scale deforestation of the Amazon, thereby further intensifying the problems of global warming. Indeed, recent scientific research suggests that the diversion of land to growing biofuel crops can produce an enormous 'CO2 debt' from the use of machinery and fertilisers, the release of carbon from the soil and the loss of CO_2 sequestration by trees and other plants that have been cleared for cultivation.

Yet, as long as government subsidies remain in the US and elsewhere, and world oil prices remain high, biofuel production is likely to continue to be encouraged despite the evident problems. And it will continue to have adverse effects on global food production and availability.

The Neglect of Agriculture

Third, the impact of policy neglect of agriculture over the past two decades is finally being felt. The prolonged agrarian crisis in many parts of the developing world has been largely a policy-determined crisis. Once again, even international officials are now admitting what has been obvious to independent observers for several years. FAO Director-General Jacques Diouf has admitted that the crisis had been building for decades: 'The situation we are in is the result of inappropriate policies over the past 20 years.'

Increases in global prices of food are likely to be exploited by large agribusiness based in the North rather than benefiting farmers in low-income countries.

These inappropriate policies have several aspects, but they all result from the basic neoliberal open market-oriented framework that has governed most economic policy making over the past two decades. One major element has been the lack of public investment in agriculture and in agricultural research. This has been associated with low to poor yield increases, especially in tropical agriculture, and falling productivity of land. Greater trade openness and market orientation of farmers have led to shifts in acreage from food crops to cash crops that have increasingly relied on purchased inputs. But both public provision and government regulation of input provision have been progressively reduced, leaving farmers at the mercy of large seed and fertiliser companies and input dealers and allowing input prices to increase quite sharply. There have also been attempts in most developing countries to reduce subsidies to farmers in the form of lower power and water prices, thus adding to cultivation costs.

The lack of attention to relevant agricultural research and extension by public bodies has denied farmers access to necessary knowledge. It has also been associated with other problems such as the excessive use of ground water in cultivation; inadequate attention to preserving or regenerating land and soil quality; and the over-use of chemical inputs that have long-run implications for both safety and productivity. Similarly, the ecological implications of both pollution and climate change, including desertification and loss of cultivable land, are issues that have been highlighted by analysts but largely ignored by policy makers in most countries.

It is often assumed that rising food prices automatically benefit farmers, but this is far from the case.

Reversing these processes is possible, and of course essential, but all this will take time and also will require substantial public investment. So until then, global supply conditions are likely to remain problematic. And meanwhile, increases in global prices of food are likely to be exploited by large agribusinesses based in the North rather than benefiting farmers in low-income countries.

There are also issues related to the loss of cultivable land because of industrialisation. Predictably, this has been most rapid in recent times in fast-growing Asia, but that is also because the process was already more advanced in the more industrialised regions of Latin America. For example, in Vietnam it is estimated that around 40,000 hectares of rice paddies are lost every year to urban construction, industrial zones and roads. In Thailand, the amount of land under cultivation dropped by more than 13% between 1995 and 2005.

Climate Change Is In Need of Attention

Fourth, there is the impact of recent climate change, which has caused poor harvests in different ways, ranging from droughts in Canada and Australia to excessive rain in parts of the US. It is projected that warmer and earlier growing seasons will increase crop susceptibility to pests and viruses, which are expected to proliferate as a direct result of rising temperatures. Some more arid regions are already more drought-prone and in danger of desertification. The rapid melting of glaciers in Asia is of huge consequence to China and India, where important rivers such as the Yangtze, Yellow and Ganges are fed by such glaciers. This will deprive the hinterland of much-needed irrigation water for wheat and rice crops during dry seasons, which is of global significance since China and India together produce more than half the world's wheat and rice. Once again, official policy has been tardy in considering such problems, much less addressing them.

Changes in Market Structure

Fifth, there is the impact of changes in market structure which allow for greater international speculation in commodities. It is often assumed that rising food prices automatically benefit farmers, but this is far from the case, especially as the global food trade has become more concentrated and vertically integrated. A small number of agribusiness companies worldwide increasingly control all aspects of cultivation and distribution, from supplying inputs to farmers to buying crops and even, in some cases, retail food distribution. This means that marketing margins are large and increasing, so that direct producers do not get the benefits of increases except with a time lag and even then not to the full extent. This concentration also enables greater speculation in food, with more centralised storage.

It is probably not a coincidence that this has happened over the same period that governments across the developing world in particular (with the notable exception of China) have reduced public holding of food stocks. The US Department of Agriculture estimates that global stock holding of wheat is at its lowest level [since the late 1970s], despite substantially increased world demand. It should be noted that the same multilateral donors (the IMF and the World Bank) whose representatives are now breast-beating about the food crisis have earlier played a major role in this reduction of state involvement, by encouraging or forcing developing-country governments to reduce 'wasteful' and 'expensive' holding of food grain stocks.

This has inevitably reduced the capacity of public intervention to prevent speculative activity from dominating markets and prices. And because public food reserves necessarily take time to build, they cannot quickly be created to ensure a reduction of speculation-induced price rises. The point has been made bluntly, if belatedly, by Jose Graziano, FAO's Regional Representative for Latin America and the Caribbean: 'The crisis is a speculative attack and it will last ... Speculative attacks become possible when you have low reserves.'

The point is that such speculation is not likely to dissipate any time soon. As the global financial system remains fragile with the continuing implosion of the US housing finance market, investors will continue to search for other avenues of investment to make up their losses and find new sources of profit. Commodity speculation has increasingly emerged as an important area for such financial investment. Such speculation by large banks and financial companies explains at least partly why the very recent period has seen such sharp hikes in price. Once again, government policies, especially with respect to the financial sector, are largely responsible for this, since financial deregulation has allowed many more complex forms of speculative activity that affect trade in commodities.

The Role of Private Trade

The role played by private traders and speculators has been especially evident in countries where aggregate domestic supply has been adequate to meet demand but there has not been enough in the hands of the public agencies. Thus in India, private trade played a role in pushing up prices of essential items even though there was no absolute shortage in aggregate terms, because the public agency had not procured enough to dampen market expectations of price rises.

So it is clear that the entire process that has led to the current food crisis has been largely policy-driven, which is probably good news because it means that policies can also reverse the process. But it is important for governments to recognise the precise role played by specific policies and think strategically on how to change them in a progressive and sustainable manner, rather than simply engage in knee-jerk reactions.

Unfortunately, though, it seems that knee-jerk responses are dominating at present. Of course, some of these are necessary to deal with the immediate crisis and ensure access to food especially for the poor. Of 58 countries whose reactions are tracked by the World Bank, 48 have imposed price controls, consumer subsidies, export restrictions or lower tariffs. But another response has been to slash import duties: at least 24 nations have reduced duties and value-added taxes on food items and allowed cheaper imports. Many countries are restricting or prohibiting exports, especially of rice or wheat. These include Egypt, Argentina, Kazakhstan, Cambodia, India and China. Meanwhile, net importers, often poor countries in Asia and Africa, are scrambling to secure supply contracts as the domestic production of food staples cannot meet consumption requirements.

Meanwhile, governments are once again turning their attention to the need to maintain public food stocks. In January [2008], the Malaysian government announced that it would create a new agency to stock up on oil, rice and other items. Other countries in Asia are also busy stockpiling grain. The Indian government has put fresh energy into ensuring that the public agency procures enough wheat from the recent harvest to ensure more than adequate buffer stock.

Another fallout of the food crisis is the greater willingness of some governments to consider genetically modified [GM] crop production. Thus, the Mexican government, which had banned GM crops for a long time, is now considering lifting the ban on genetically modified corn. It is possible that similar bans in the European Union and some countries of Africa could also be reconsidered if the aggregate shortages continue.

Speculation Has Driven Up Food Prices and Created Shortages

Beat Balzli and Frank Hornig

Beat Balzli and Frank Hornig are journalists with Spiegel *Magazine.*

Not long ago, Dwight Anderson welcomed reporters with open arms. He liked to entertain them with stories from the world of big money. Anderson is a New York hedge fund manager, and as recently as last October [2007] he would talk with enthusiasm about his visits to Malaysian palm-oil plantations and Brazilian grain farms. "You could clearly see how supply was getting tight," he said.

In mid-2006 Anderson was touting the "extraordinary profitability" of field crops from corn to soybeans. He was convinced that rising worldwide hunger would be synonymous with highly profitable—and dead-certain—investment bargains.

In search of new investments, Anderson sends dozens of his employees to visit agricultural regions around the world. Back in New York, at his company's headquarters on the 27th floor of an office building high above Park Avenue, they bet on agricultural markets from Peru to Vietnam.

But in the towers above Manhattan's urban canyons, it's easy to lose touch with the ground. Hedge fund manager John Paulson was recently celebrated for achieving a record annual profit of $3.7 billion. Those who work in this environment have only one rule: Don't disappoint profit-hungry investors.

"I'm constantly wired," Anderson used to say, back when he talked to journalists. His nickname in the industry is the

"Commodities King," and his Ospraie hedge fund is the world's largest. These days, though, Anderson avoids the media. He's even kept his face out of the media by buying up rights to all photos of himself on the market. His spokesman is now paid, mainly, to say nothing.

A Broken Market?

There are plenty of questions to ask Anderson, though—in particular about the role of international investors in the current spike in the price of staple food. Not only is there talk that investors have profited from desperate hunger in Honduras, the Philippines and Bangladesh; critics also wonder if commodity speculators are making the crisis worse.

[In April 2008] in Washington, DC, a regulatory body called the Commodity Futures Trading Commission held public hearings on this very question. Farmers and food producers argued that the market was "broken," suggesting that the steep rise in the price of staple crops was hurting everyone—farmers as well as the people they feed. "The market is broken, it's out of whack," said Billy Dunavant, head of a cotton-producing firm in the United States, at the . . . hearing.

Regulators on the commission warned against government intervention, and no doubt fund managers like Anderson would, too. But the crisis keeps deteriorating. India and Vietnam have imposed export bans on ordinary rice. Indonesia is following suit. According to the United Nations, North Korea is on the brink of a humanitarian crisis. After unrest shook countries from Egypt and Uzbekistan to Bangladesh, thousands of South Africans took to the streets of Johannesburg last Thursday [April 17, 2008] to protest high food prices. In Haiti, the prime minister was fired after riots over the price of rice.

Biofuels and global warming have been blamed for shortages driving up the price of food, and both trends have played their role. The planet's grain reserves are almost empty for a number of reasons, including global population growth and greater prosperity in some countries like India. Feed corn is in short supply because industrialized nations have used it for ethanol. Droughts—in Australia, for example—have devastated rice and wheat harvests. Wheat reserves worldwide are only sufficient right now to cover about 60 days of demand.

This helps to explain why commodity prices have rallied since early 2006, with the price of rice ballooning 217 percent, wheat 136 percent, corn 125 percent and soybeans 107 percent.

But classic supply and demand theory offers only a partial explanation. Sudden price hikes since last January have been alarming. The UN [United Nations] estimates that at least $500 million in immediate aid will be needed by May [2008] to avoid serious famines. Agricultural scientists at the world body's Educational, Scientific and Cultural Organization (UNESCO) have presented a report on the world food crisis. And criticism is growing that hedge funds, index funds, pension funds and investment banks bear part of the blame.

The History of Futures

Commodity speculation spread long ago from standard products like oil and gold to anything edible and available for trade on the Chicago Futures Exchange. These days there are futures contracts for everything from wheat to oranges to pork bellies. The futures market is a traditional tool for farmers to sell their harvests ahead of time. In a futures contract, quantities, prices and delivery dates are fixed, sometimes even before crops have been planted. Futures contracts allow farmers and grain wholesalers a measure of protection against adverse weather conditions and excessive price fluctuations. They can also help a farmer plan how much to plant for a given year.

But now speculators are taking advantage of this mechanism. They can buy futures contracts for wheat, for example, at a low price, betting that the price will go up. If the price of the grain rises by the agreed delivery date, they profit.

What is happening now in the wheat market is unprecedented ... [C]apitalism is literally consuming itself.

Some experts now believe these investors have taken over the market, buying futures at unprecedented levels and driving up short-term prices. [Between August 2007 and April 2008] this mechanism has led to a doubling in the price of rice—including the 500,000 tons that the Philippine government plans to buy in early May [2008] to address its own shortage.

Greg Warner has worked in the grain wholesaling business for more than two decades. His office sits a block away from the Chicago Futures Exchange. He's an analyst with the firm AgResource, and he says what is happening now in the wheat market is unprecedented.

"What we normally have is a predictable group of sellers and buyers—mainly farmers and silo operators," he says. But the landscape has changed since the influx of large index funds. Fund managers seek to maximize their profits using futures contracts, and prices, says Warner, "keep climbing up and up."

He's calculated that financial investors now hold the rights to two complete annual harvests of a type of grain traded in Chicago called "soft red winter wheat."

Warner is stunned by such developments. He sees them as evidence that capitalism is literally consuming itself.

This Practice Needs an Ethical Discussion

Even the Commodity Futures Trading Commission in Washington has recognized the potentially explosive nature of the issue. For [the] hearing, the commission called not just on farmers but also on representatives of investment bank Goldman Sachs and major investors like Pimco and AIG to testify. One member of the commission, Bart Chilton, backed away from regulating investors, saying, "These markets have to work for all the participants. If you don't have speculators in the markets, there's no liquidity and you don't have a market." And the editor of a commodities newsletter, Dennis Gartman, flat-out denied that speculators were to blame.

"It is an election year," he said. "To think you won't have senators and congressmen blaming high prices of things on speculators is naive."

But some basic market rules seem to have stopped working. "The enormous influx of capital has resulted in the futures markets no longer reflecting supply and demand," says Todd Kemp of the US National Grain and Feed Association. Ironically, investors have placed their wildest bets on staple foods. Information about supply bottlenecks and famines at the other end of the world is not noted on market quotations.

A commodities dealer named Christoph Eibl soberly concludes that financial managers just want to "benefit from the scarcity of these commodities." Eibl's Stuttgart-based investment firm, Tiberius, manages $1.6 billion. His in-house experts estimate that hundreds of billions of dollars have flowed into the futures sector as a whole within the last five years, much of it for agricultural commodities. Eibl admits the whole thing demands an "ethical discussion." Some futures traders argue that they don't cause prices to rise in the real world because as a rule they never take delivery of a given crop—other parts of the economy control the actual street price. But futures prices affect real-world behavior (such as inventory hoarding), and Eibl says that buying futures in rice, for example, "eventually causes consumer prices to rise in developing countries like Haiti."

Voices like Eibl's have been rare until now, perhaps because a comparable commodities boom has never existed before. Experts are already discussing what they call a "super cycle," set off by constantly growing demand in China, and by farmers unable, in the long term, to keep up with that demand as they sow their seed and harvest their crops. The planet has only a finite amount of land for farming.

The upshot is that more and more small investors are jumping on the commodities bandwagon. Many investors, not unlike hedge fund managers, seek diversification in their portfolios, partly through investment in agricultural commodities. From the standpoint of these investors, poor harvests that drive up prices are only good for their portfolios. Many investors either don't care or are simply oblivious to the fact that by investing in the global casino, they could be gambling away the daily food supply of the world's poorest people.

The Career Gamblers

Andreas Grünewald is a star among small investors in Germany. He launched his Munich Investment Club (MIC), together with eight fellow students and his grandfather, in 1989 with about $24,000 in initial capital. Grünewald, a business school graduate, now manages more than $80 million for the MIC's 2,500 members.

Commodities are a big issue for Grünewald. "They are the megatrend of the decade," he says. His portfolio in this sector is already worth about $24 million. According to Grünewald, this is only the start.

Riots because of exploding rice prices? Aid organizations in a state of high alert? None of this matters much to . . . apostles of profit.

Grünewald says he wants to "remain broadly invested" in water and agricultural commodities, in particular, and "to expand those investments if possible." He has already placed his bets on oranges, sugar and corn on the futures exchanges. His bet on wheat alone has produced a handsome profit of 93 percent to date.

Grünewald has already planned his next step. "Rice is another interesting topic that could complement our portfolio very effectively," he says. Scruples are in short supply in Grünewald's investment club.

"Most of our members tend to be passive and profit-oriented," he admits. At MIC's national events, few people bring up the social consequences of his investment tips. Riots because of exploding rice prices? Aid organizations in a state of high alert? None of this matters much to the preferred suppliers and apostles of profit in the small investor community. The finance industry regularly introduces new investment "products" for every sexy sector, no matter how questionable.

Financial giant ABN Amro has been especially adept at turning a profit in the current market. As a provider of commodities-investment products for private investors, ABN Amro ... became the first bank to offer certificates allowing small investors to place bets on rising rice prices on the Chicago Futures Exchange.

The bank's marketing department has reacted with cold precision to headlines about famine around the world. Two weeks ago, when experts warned of an impending hunger crisis and the political instability associated with it, ABN Amro introduced a new ad campaign on its website. As India imposes a ban on rice exports, the ad said, world rice supplies have declined to a minimum: Now ABN Amro was making it possible, for the first time, to invest in Asia's most important basic food product.

Unveiling an investment product during a supply bottleneck that has since led to riots? Are ABN Amro's bankers really such clichéd, unscrupulous bean counters? "We are aware of the current discussions relating to agricultural commodities," says Önder Ciftci, head of ABN Amro's German certifi-

cate business. But he's not interested in a discussion of
"We make the drills, but others have to do the drilli
says.

ABN Amro has, in fact, drilled into substantial so
profit. In the space of only three weeks, investors ra
turns of more than 20 percent. The number of futur
tracts traded in Chicago has skyrocketed.

No Food at All?

Jim Rogers, the former business partner of legendary f
and philanthropist George Soros, is perhaps the best
investor in broad-based commodity funds. He started
his money to commodities in the 1990s. On his trips
the world, he came to realize that almost everythir
nickel to cacao, was in short supply in a globalized ec

He's laid bets on rising prices ever since. This has
impact on the entire industry, because Rogers' Inter
Commodities Index is a benchmark for countless fund
moneymaking machines have attracted billions in inv
in recent years, and some of that money has been
into futures contracts, heating up prices even further.

But now Rogers, of all people, is warning: "Unle
thing happens soon, we will see people not getting an
all, at any price. This is the sort of thing we read abou
tory books, but now I'm afraid that it could happen

From his perspective, though, the calamity is not
of investors like him, but of developing countries' p
like imposing export bans and capping prices. This
farmers, who face rising costs of necessary items like
fertilizer, of any incentive to produce more rice.

"I think this attitude is morally reprehensible," :
ers. "These governments would rather let people st;
allow prices to rise naturally." Removing price con
says, is the only way to increase rice production le
again.

A Lack of Regulation 1
Caused the Food Crisi:

Gretchen Gordon

*Gretchen Gordon is a fellow at Food Fir
Development Policy.*

You wouldn't know it by watching (
C-SPAN, but if you turn on the 1
global food system is in crisis. Food p
rocketed, in some cases 80%. Food p
Italy to Yemen have begun capturing wi
policymakers are scrambling to point fi
prits—everything from climate change,
dollar and the biofuels boom, to meat
these factors have played a part in the
blame game is also allowing one culpr
tagonist in this story—to get away wit
It's a character you might have heard of
that little unfortunate sub-prime mortg
deregulation.

Pundits have spent a fair amount
the deregulated financial markets that
crisis. But the regulatory state of global
something most policymakers, let alon
given much of a thought. In many ways
are similar: global markets, deregulation
tal don't mix well. However, in two key
differ substantially: the scale of deregula
consequences.

bets on oranges, sugar and corn on the futures exchanges. His bet on wheat alone has produced a handsome profit of 93 percent to date.

Grünewald has already planned his next step. "Rice is another interesting topic that could complement our portfolio very effectively," he says. Scruples are in short supply in Grünewald's investment club.

"Most of our members tend to be passive and profit-oriented," he admits. At MIC's national events, few people bring up the social consequences of his investment tips. Riots because of exploding rice prices? Aid organizations in a state of high alert? None of this matters much to the preferred suppliers and apostles of profit in the small investor community. The finance industry regularly introduces new investment "products" for every sexy sector, no matter how questionable.

Financial giant ABN Amro has been especially adept at turning a profit in the current market. As a provider of commodities-investment products for private investors, ABN Amro . . . became the first bank to offer certificates allowing small investors to place bets on rising rice prices on the Chicago Futures Exchange.

The bank's marketing department has reacted with cold precision to headlines about famine around the world. Two weeks ago, when experts warned of an impending hunger crisis and the political instability associated with it, ABN Amro introduced a new ad campaign on its website. As India imposes a ban on rice exports, the ad said, world rice supplies have declined to a minimum: Now ABN Amro was making it possible, for the first time, to invest in Asia's most important basic food product.

Unveiling an investment product during a supply bottleneck that has since led to riots? Are ABN Amro's bankers really such clichéd, unscrupulous bean counters? "We are aware of the current discussions relating to agricultural commodities," says Önder Ciftci, head of ABN Amro's German certificate business. But he's not interested in a discussion of ethics. "We make the drills, but others have to do the drilling," he says.

ABN Amro has, in fact, drilled into substantial source of profit. In the space of only three weeks, investors raked returns of more than 20 percent. The number of futures contracts traded in Chicago has skyrocketed.

No Food at All?

Jim Rogers, the former business partner of legendary financier and philanthropist George Soros, is perhaps the best-known investor in broad-based commodity funds. He started shifting his money to commodities in the 1990s. On his trips around the world, he came to realize that almost everything, from nickel to cacao, was in short supply in a globalized economy.

He's laid bets on rising prices ever since. This has had an impact on the entire industry, because Rogers' International Commodities Index is a benchmark for countless funds. These moneymaking machines have attracted billions in investments in recent years, and some of that money has been pumped into futures contracts, heating up prices even further.

But now Rogers, of all people, is warning: "Unless something happens soon, we will see people not getting any food at all, at any price. This is the sort of thing we read about in history books, but now I'm afraid that it could happen again."

From his perspective, though, the calamity is not the fault of investors like him, but of developing countries' policies— like imposing export bans and capping prices. This deprives farmers, who face rising costs of necessary items like fuel and fertilizer, of any incentive to produce more rice.

"I think this attitude is morally reprehensible," says Rogers. "These governments would rather let people starve than allow prices to rise naturally." Removing price controls, he says, is the only way to increase rice production levels once again.

Farmers, after all, wouldn't give away their rice to the poor, says Rogers. But he fails to explain how the poor should pay the higher prices in the first place. Perhaps it's up to politicians?

A Lack of Regulation Has Caused the Food Crisis

Gretchen Gordon

Gretchen Gordon is a fellow at Food First/Institute for Food and Development Policy.

You wouldn't know it by watching Congressional debate on C-SPAN, but if you turn on the news, it's clear that the global food system is in crisis. Food prices globally have skyrocketed, in some cases 80%. Food protests and riots from Italy to Yemen have begun capturing worldwide attention, and policymakers are scrambling to point fingers at a litany of culprits—everything from climate change, high oil prices, a weak dollar and the biofuels boom, to meat eaters in China. All of these factors have played a part in the current crisis, but the blame game is also allowing one culprit—the principle protagonist in this story—to get away with not even a mention. It's a character you might have heard of recently for its role in that little unfortunate sub-prime mortgage mess. That's right, deregulation.

Pundits have spent a fair amount of air time describing the deregulated financial markets that sparked the mortgage crisis. But the regulatory state of global agricultural markets is something most policymakers, let alone consumers, haven't given much of a thought. In many ways the dynamics at play are similar: global markets, deregulation and speculative capital don't mix well. However, in two key regards, these markets differ substantially: the scale of deregulation, and the scale of consequences.

The Scale of Deregulation

First, let's look at the scale of deregulation. Deregulation in agricultural markets, like economic deregulation in many sectors, reached full tilt in the eighties and nineties. Trade and development economists preached the wonders of open markets, unfettered production, and industrial agriculture. The World Bank and International Monetary Fund conditioned loan policies on the elimination of government intervention in agricultural markets. Global commodity agreements, price supports, and other mechanisms which helped keep global supplies and prices stable were dismantled. The World Trade Organization's Agreement on Agriculture, together with multilateral and bilateral agreements including the North American Free Trade Agreement (NAFTA), slashed agricultural tariffs in the developing world, and opened up markets for a growing global agribusiness industry.

In the U.S., the 1996 Farm Bill eliminated the last vestiges of domestic price supports for most commodities and replaced them with a massive system of subsidies—the only thing left to prop up a farm economy in perpetual crisis. Market liberalization and the dumping of cheap commodities swamped small farmers here and abroad, pricing them out of local markets. Cheap feed crops fueled industrial livestock production, increasing meat consumption and driving out small producers. The few independent farmers who stayed in farming shifted production to a few commodities including corn and soy that can be stored and shipped to distant markets.

The impact of all this deregulation was to replace local market access for the majority of small producers with global market access for a few global producers. Thanks to nonexistent anti-trust enforcement and rampant vertical integration, we've reached a level of concentration in our global agriculture system that would make Standard Oil blush. Three companies—Cargill, Archer Daniels Midland [ADM] and

Bunge—control the vast majority of global grain trading, while Monsanto controls more than one-fifth of the global market in seeds. Consumers from Sioux City to Soweto are more and more dependent on fewer and fewer producers. By eliminating the breadth and diversity of the system, we've eliminated its ability to withstand shock or manipulation.

Perhaps the greatest evidence of the scale of deregulation of the world agricultural market is the liquidation of reliable grain reserves. Though we've impressively deregulated financial markets, the Federal Reserve and central bankers across the globe still maintain the ability to soften the spikes and plunges of our monetary system. Not so in food markets. For centuries grain reserves have been an essential component of functioning food systems. When prices are high grain reserves can be released on the market, bringing prices down. When prices are low, reserve systems buy up grain, bringing prices back up. In the last two decades, however, the U.S. and most other governments have let reserve systems wither, placing full faith in the free market to self-correct, and eliminating their last emergency response mechanism.

Commodities, Farmland, and Biofuels

Remember the mortgage crisis? [The subprime mortgage crisis which began in late 2006] After the mortgage crisis, investors needed a new place to put their money. So they pumped it into commodities, farmland, and the new biofuels boom. Before it became a favorite climate savior, the idea of growing crops for ethanol was sold to U.S. farmers as a way to bail out the rural crisis and channel excess supply, while letting the free market continue to dictate prices. Seeing the volatility in the market and knowing that grain reserves were depleted, the grain traders started withholding supply in hopes of higher prices, playing off currency differentials, and shifting production and investments in search of greater returns. In many cases speculative fear caused the scarcity price effect, more than actual shortage. Investors started hedging their bets, buying grain futures, and driving up prices even more. Though the biofuels boom has exacerbated speculation and high prices, that boom wouldn't have been possible without a deregulated global market.

While farmers in the U.S. may have seen the price for a bushel of corn go from $2 to $6 [between 2006 and 2008], their inputs, everything from seeds to fertilizer to diesel for tractors, have also multiplied, significantly deflating any increase in income. The difference between a short windfall and long term profit shift is being able to pass on price increases to consumers, something only the big guys have the market power to do. Cargill's third-quarter profits have increased over 86%. General Mills' are up 61%, and Monsanto's are up 45%.

What we're seeing right now—skyrocketing food prices and growing hunger—are still the effects of the [economic] boom.

The Cargills and ADMs of the world are traders—similar to financial traders—but in livestock and commodity futures. In an un-regulated global market they've gained enough market share that through buying and selling, they can play off both supply and demand. And their actions can set the direction of global prices. They can send shockwaves through the entire system. Now the unregulated market runs on the principle that capital will work in its best interest, and it's not in agribusiness' best interest to tank the entire agricultural system. But in the recent corn and soy spike, even the multinational livestock producers and food companies have begun to feel the sting. When the stakes get to a certain level, the gambler can make decisions that are against his own self-interest.

The Consequences of Deregulation

So that brings us to the second key difference between the housing crisis and the food crisis: the scale of consequences. When a housing bubble inflates till it pops, people lose their homes. But when a food bubble grows till it bursts, people starve.

The problem with booms is they're almost inevitably followed by busts. Worse news is that what we're seeing right now—skyrocketing food prices and growing hunger—are still the effects of the boom. If the weather turns bad, commodity prices could still double over the next few months. But with the stability of the food and agriculture system left up to the whims of mother nature's next crop yield, or how Cargill, ADM and the venture capitalists spin the roulette wheel, the bust is in the making. If the rural farm economy tanks, we're set to see farm foreclosures, another banking crisis, and global hunger that will make the sub-prime mortgage effects look like a drop in the bucket.

So what are world leaders doing about this impending crisis? Politicians like George [W.] Bush and Gordon Brown, in lockstep with the World Trade Organization and the World Bank, are mainly proposing two solutions to the food crisis: food aid, and increased free trade in industrial agriculture. Agribusiness is positioned to cash in on the perceived need to ramp up production globally and to tear down remaining trade barriers. And Monsanto already has policymakers parroting its line of increasing efficiency and yields through investments in genetic engineering and high-tech inputs.

The unregulated free market has proven itself the gambling addict that it is—incapable of self control.

The architects of the failed free market are now prescribing more of the same, and policymakers are swallowing it part and parcel. However, rather than solutions to the problems of the global agricultural system, these are root causes. While urgent measures need to be taken to address acute hunger in places like African countries and Haiti, Bush's $200 million food aid proposal is equivalent to his $300 tax return in terms of actually fixing economic malfunction. At its root, hunger is not about lack of food, it's about poverty and inequity, and the inability to access available food. Just as if middle class Americans had better paying jobs, they wouldn't need a tax refund; if small farmers in Africa had access to land and local markets they wouldn't need food aid. Another gross injustice of our food aid policy is the requirement that the majority of it be purchased and shipped from the U.S. rather than bought from local producers. Where's that food aid going to come from—big agribusiness. Meanwhile, African producers will once again be denied income and shut out of their local market.

Back on C-SPAN, there's a $280 billion Farm Bill mired in political wrangling in the Senate. Unfortunately, those billions don't go to help fix this broken food and farming system. What they do instead is give more biofuels tax breaks and more subsidies for agribusiness. But no provisions for reserves . . . No price management mechanisms . . . No regulation. Once again corporate lobbyists have worked hard for their paychecks.

It is long past time we re-claim a rational economic and agriculture policy in this country and globally, before it's too late. The unregulated free market has proven itself the gambling addict that it is—incapable of self control. We saw it in the sub-prime mortgage crisis and we're seeing it in the current food crisis. The venture capitalists and the ADMs and Cargills have bet both the house and the farm. Now global leaders have a choice: they can either regulate, or leave the fate of our economic and food systems to the next roll of the dice.

Food Cannot Be Globalized Like Other Commodities

Bruce Stokes

Bruce Stokes is the international economics columnist for the National Journal, *and he works on the Pew Research Center's Global Attitudes Project.*

Robert Zoellick, head of the World Bank, warns that the unfolding food crisis could force 100 million people deeper into destitution and set back efforts to reduce world poverty by seven years.

In the midst of this crisis, the immediate humanitarian challenge is to feed the hungry. But the suddenness and breadth of the emergency has raised fundamental questions about the future of agricultural policy that will drive debates in Washington and other world capitals for years to come. The questions being posed about agricultural policies are complex and hard to answer.

Was it a mistake over the past generation to increasingly trust market forces to feed the world? Or are the problems that bedevil farmers today the residue of continued government interference in agricultural markets? Are current food prices a problem or the ultimate solution to future food needs? Does the world food system suffer from too much globalization or not enough?

In the search for answers to these questions, Washington is a Tower of Babel. Partisans of all stripes have seized on the crisis to justify their long-standing ideological positions on agriculture. Free-market proponents support a swift completion of the Doha Round of multilateral trade negotiations, which would cut American and European farm subsidies and allow developing countries to increase their food exports to rich countries. "The solution is to break the Doha Development Agenda impasse in 2008," Zoellick said in April.

Some recent experience bolsters this argument. Since the early 1970s, when the world last endured a food crisis, production has soared, to the point that, until a few years ago, food experts worried that grain prices were too low to adequately reward farmers' efforts. The global trade in grain delivered cheap food to the poor in the burgeoning cities of the developing world. Malnutrition rates fell in many parts of the globe.

But skeptics contend that leaving the supply of food solely to the market's whims is a mistake. "The mindless liberalization mentality at the World Bank, the U.S. Agency for International Development, and among my fellow economists misses the fact that food is a biological necessity as well as a commodity," said Peter Timmer, a visiting professor at Stanford University's Program on Food Security and the Environment.

With its short-term orientation, the free market has frequently failed the long-term interests of consumers around the world, critics contend. Governments have been pulling back from investing in the underlying infrastructure that supports agriculture. As a result, funding has atrophied for the development of new high-yielding seeds, for the building of better farm-to-market roads, and for loans to small cultivators. International grain traders and speculators have gained unprecedented influence over commodity markets. And world grain stocks have been allowed to dwindle to modern lows.

The proper balance between government and the private sector will be at the center of the emerging debate over agriculture.

These changes in the worldwide food market are compounded by what economists like to call "externalities," factors that are not susceptible to market discipline but that are rapidly shaping the future of agriculture: rising energy prices, water shortages, and, ultimately, climate change.

"We are looking at diminishing returns in a number of areas," said Lester Brown, president of the Earth Policy Institute in Washington. "We spend a lot of money on research, with disappointing results. We are using more fertilizer, but that does not increase yields. We look [for] but don't find much new water."

In the face of these challenges, said Gawain Kripke, director of policy and research at Oxfam America, "there are no silver bullets. We need a matrix of solutions."

The proper balance between government and the private sector will be at the center of the emerging debate over agriculture. "Some public intervention is needed," said Kimberly Elliott, a senior fellow at the Center for Global Development in Washington. "The question is, what is the right intervention?"

The ultimate matrix may include less direct government interference in the short-term workings of global food markets through subsidies and tariffs, coupled with greater government responsibility for providing a strategic grain reserve, funding basic research, and stewarding the environment to help compensate for inevitable market hiccups and externalities that can cripple food production.

Change in Fortunes

Just a decade ago, humanity's age-old race to stay one step ahead of famine seemed finally won. Grain supplies were bountiful and growing. Food prices were low.

Then, world cereals production fell two years in a row, thanks in part to bad weather. This falloff came at a time of record low food stocks. With poor harvests and low reserves, the market was vulnerable to shocks that could send prices spiraling. That is just what happened. Despite a rebound in harvests in 2007, the U.S. diverted most of the extra corn it raised into making ethanol to fuel its cars and trucks. U.S. corn prices tripled. And, with cropland being diverted from wheat to corn production, wheat prices more than doubled.

In the midst of so much want, it may seem heartless to question whether high food prices help or hurt the poor.

In October 2007, spooked by mushrooming food prices, India, one of the world's largest exporters of rice, banned most of its rice shipments. Vietnam followed with export restrictions in January 2008.

Rice prices rose sharply.

Not surprisingly, consumers rapidly felt the pain in America, yes, but all over the world, too. Food prices rose 11.4 percent in Indonesia, 11.6 percent in Guatemala, and 18.3 percent in Botswana in a year. In such societies, where the poor may spend more than half of their income on food, this was a severe additional burden.

Nevertheless, a bit of light has appeared on the horizon. Higher prices have already spurred farmers around the world to plant more this spring. And the U.N. [United Nations] Food and Agriculture Organization [FAO] expects harvests to improve this year. World prices have already begun to fall from their recent highs as a result. Still, over the next decade, experts predict that crop prices will remain well above the mean for the past decade. The days of cheap food may be over.

High Prices: Problem or Solution?

In the midst of so much want, it may seem heartless to question whether high food prices help or hurt the poor. But that is exactly the debate raging among development economists.

Higher prices reward farmers, who receive more for their harvests, and punish consumers, who must pay more to feed their families. Many people in the poorest parts of the world—Africa, Asia, and Latin America—sell more food than they consume.

A recent FAO study found that half of the households in Madagascar and two in five households in Ghana, all classified as extremely poor, were net sellers of food and stood to benefit from higher prices. A recent Carnegie Endowment study of India found that "the poorest households and the most disadvantaged groups saw the largest gains" from a rise in rice prices, thanks to greater demand for their land and their low-skilled labor to produce that staple.

But the vast majority of poor households in Bangladesh and Pakistan are net *buyers* of food. Overall, conclude World Bank economists Maros Ivanic and Will Martin, in a recent paper, "even though many rural households gain from higher food prices, the overall impact on poverty remains negative."

The fact is, higher prices create both losers and winners, even among the poor. And the distribution of winners and losers varies from country to country. Nor is the market for food the same from country to country. Thus, warned Sandra Polaski, director of the Trade, Equity, and Development Program at the Carnegie Endowment, generalizing from the experience of particular countries about the effects of food price increases on poverty can lead to incorrect one-size-fits-all policy prescriptions. Today's food crisis is highly differentiated, requiring tailored solutions.

Too Much Globalization

Current food shortages are also a reminder that what globalization gives, it can take away.

Since the food emergency in the early 1970s, world trade in agricultural products has increased severalfold. The globalization theory was that increased trade in food crops would lead to more production at lower prices. The notion that countries had to be self-sustaining in agriculture would fade away.

But the current crisis suggests to some critics that globalization may not have worked as intended. "Removal of tariff barriers has allowed a handful of northern countries to capture Third World markets by dumping heavily subsidized commodities while undermining local food production," said Anuradha Mittal, executive director of the Oakland Institute, a California-based think tank that advocates food sovereignty.

Globalization . . . encouraged a more efficient food market, in which grain moved around the world rapidly.

The Doha Round of trade talks threatens to make this situation worse, the critics contend. To safeguard their food security, some developing countries demand the right to exempt "special products" from tariff cuts, with each country's list targeted to its individual needs. In addition, they want to slow unexpected surges of food imports.

"Let's not put policies in place that make the current situation worse," said Polaski, who argues that farming in the developing world can be nurtured only behind trade barriers. "You can't do it in the face of global competition," she said.

Trade liberalization is part of a broader set of market-oriented economic reforms that the World Bank and International Monetary Fund began to impose on many developing countries in the 1980s in return for loans. These reforms were intended to balance governmental budgets. But critics complain that they often harmed farmers. In 14 developing countries, farm spending fell from an average of 6.9 percent of gross domestic product in 1980 to 4 percent in 2004, according to a recent World Bank survey.

Globalization also encouraged a more efficient food market, in which grain moved around the world rapidly. Surpluses in one region easily replenished shortages in another. There seemed little need to maintain large, costly grain reserves. China, the European Union, and the United States let their food stocks dwindle as a result.

Recent price volatility suggests that the global food system now lacks flexibility because food stocks declined too far. In 2007, reserves equaled 54 days of world consumption, down from a high of 130 days in 1986.

The United States and other countries maintain strategic petroleum reserves. Through the International Energy Agency in Paris, they have agreements to share supplies during an emergency. So why not a strategic grain reserve?

It is a question of cost and control. American and European taxpayers have bad memories of out-of-control government spending to maintain grain and butter "mountains" in silos and warehouses. Recent rice export bans suggest that hoarding by producer nations does more harm than good—it just drives prices even higher.

With the FAO now predicting that grain prices could remain high for a decade, resulting increases in production may rebuild reserves on their own. But to be prudent, Stanford University's Timmer suggests new international incentives for producing countries to hold greater stocks, coupled with agreements on what market conditions would trigger their release. Oxfam argues for village-level cereal banks that would ensure adequate local supplies during hard times.

Globalization, driven by the theory of comparative advantage, has also encouraged agricultural specialization. "This led to the dedication of good land to export crops with food crops forced into less suitable soil, thus exacerbating food insecurity," wrote Walden Bello, a professor of sociology at the University of the Philippines, in a recent issue of *The Nation*. In years when specialty crop prices were high and food staple prices low, this was a rational trade-off for farmers to make. It was a bet that many countries are now losing.

Finally, globalization of the world food system exacerbates the effects of sudden policy shifts, such as the recent U.S. rush to use corn to increase ethanol production. In 2006, the approximately $6 billion in U.S. subsidies for ethanol production spurred demand for corn, triggering chain-reaction price rises around the world for corn, wheat, and soybeans. Never has the energy policy of a country that is not a member of OPEC had such a devastating global impact.

Not Enough Globalization

It is no surprise that defenders of globalization hold a quite different view. They contend that a stronger, more open market is part of the solution to the food crisis.

Paul Collier, a professor of economics at Oxford University and the author of the recent award-winning book *The Bottom Billion*, criticizes the seductive notion of peasant-based, food self-sufficiency as hopelessly romantic. "We laud the production style of the peasant," he wrote in a recent blog. "In manufacturing and services we grew out of this fantasy years ago, but in agriculture it continues to contaminate our policies. Unfortunately, peasant farming is generally not well suited to innovation and investment."

Trade, these globalization defenders argue, has been the salvation of consumers in poorer countries, not their bane. "If you are for self-sufficiency, you must be willing to live with high prices," wrote Dani Rodrik, a professor of international political economy at Harvard University in his blog. "If developing countries had all kept their import protection, the global supply of food would have been lower today, not higher."

Globalization advocates condemn continued government intervention in agriculture. Farm subsidies in rich countries have long boosted production there, holding down world prices and undermining market incentives for farmers in poor countries to grow more food. High industrial-country tariffs, meanwhile, have kept out food imports from developing countries. If African, Asian, and Latin American food production is to increase, U.S., European, and Japanese subsidies need to be eliminated and their tariffs slashed, the globalization advocates argue.

However the world ultimately resolves the debate about globalization, the food crisis is a reminder that market forces are notoriously shortsighted.

If they are right, the path ahead will be long. The 2008 U.S. farm bill actually increased permissible American farm payments. If high prices continue, much of that money may never get spent. But the very availability of those subsidies reduces farmers' risk, encouraging more planting. And some of the highest remaining industrial-country trade barriers apply to some of the very products, such as sugar and cotton, that farmers in developing countries may be most competitive at growing.

The Doha Round, if it is ever completed, will not significantly cut farm subsidies or import tariffs in rich countries. Doha negotiators also seem unlikely to liberalize some of the most important agricultural commerce, trade between developing countries. Cutting import barriers *between* developing countries—spurring more South-South trade—would be far more important to the economic welfare of such nations than reductions in farm support or export subsidies in developed countries, according to World Bank studies.

So if globalization is to ease food supply problems, proponents argue for more of it, not less.

Dealing With Market Breakdowns

However the world ultimately resolves the debate about globalization, the food crisis is a reminder that market forces are notoriously shortsighted and governments too often scrimp on the kinds of long-term investments that can sustain productive agriculture.

Between 1960 and 1970, thanks to the green revolution, global grain yields grew by 2.6 percent per year on average. From 1990 to 2007, the annual increase had slowed to only 1.2 percent. Apparently, the reservoir of agricultural technologies that farmers can readily rely on to boost harvests is shrinking.

Yet both the private and the public sector have failed to address this market failure. The proportion of World Bank lending devoted to agriculture has declined steadily since the 1980s, and the proportion of all foreign aid from all sources going to farmers is now only 4 percent. As a result, the seed company Monsanto spends seven times as much on research and development as the 14 international agricultural research institutes combined. And that private spending often concentrates on developing seed varieties for commercial agriculture, not for food staples that make up the diet of the very poor.

Similarly, the food production and distribution infrastructure has been given short shrift. In much of sub-Saharan Africa, concluded the World Bank in its 2008 World Development Report, poor market access was almost as important a constraint on food availability as poor rainfall. Transport costs, in part because of bad roads, account for about a third of the price that African countries pay for fertilizer. A public-private partnership to build roads and ports is needed to break these infrastructure logjams.

Oligopolies, which concentrate market share in the hands of a few companies, may be further aggravating global agricultural problems. The four largest agrochemical companies now control 60 percent of the world fertilizer market, up from 47 percent in 1997. The four largest seed firms have cornered 33 percent of the market, up from 23 percent in the same timeframe.

This concentration is also evident on the distribution side. International traders control 40 percent of the international market for coffee, which is the source of livelihood for an estimated 25 million farmers and farmworkers around the world. With greater market power, these traders can charge higher prices. The share of the retail price Americans pay for a pound of coffee beans that actually goes to the coffee-producing countries of Brazil, Colombia, Indonesia, and Vietnam has declined from about a third in the early 1990s to only about 10 percent in 2002.

"It is generally believed," the 2008 World Development Report concluded, "that when an industry's [market share] exceeds 40 percent, market competitiveness begins to decline, leading to higher spreads between what consumers pay and what producers receive for their produce." In laymen's terms, the middlemen win; consumers and farmers lose.

The global food system might well benefit from a little Teddy Roosevelt-style trustbusting.

Coping With the Externalities

A final problem with the world market for food is that it is deeply affected by those unpredictable "externalities" that the economists talk about—factors, such as weather, that are important but not easily controlled. These include:

- Population growth. Strides have been made since the last food crisis in the 1970s in slowing population growth, a major driver of food demand. In the world as a whole, the average number of children per woman has fallen from nearly five to fewer than three. Yet even as population growth slows, the sheer number of women of childbearing age has driven annual population growth: About 81 million new people appeared on the globe in 2007, far more than in the early 1970s.

  "You don't have to be an agronomist to know that if you keep adding that many mouths to feed each year, you are going to be in trouble," said Brown, of the Earth Policy Institute.

In nearly all developing countries, the number of women of reproductive age will increase between 2005 and 2015.

- Rising affluence. Higher incomes enable more people to eat higher on the food chain. The World Bank estimates that by 2030 more than a billion consumers in the developing world will have sufficient income to eat a middle-class diet. China provides a foretaste of this future. Between 1990 and 2006, per capita Chinese meat consumption grew by 140 percent, and individual milk consumption by 300 percent.

  To produce 1 pound of meat takes up to 7 pounds of grain. So with developing countries' meat consumption expected to double in a generation, demand for grain will grow much faster than population.

  Slowing such consumption may prove impossible. European and American consumers could change their diets, but large-scale reform of consumption patterns is unlikely. And for African, Asian, and Latin American consumers, eating richer diets is one of the long-sought benefits of development. The stresses on the food system associated with rising affluence will simply have to be accommodated; they probably cannot be reversed.

- Energy prices. Higher fuel prices are also likely to further complicate the market's ability to meet the food needs for both consumers and producers. It requires about 41.5 gallons of oil (in the form of fertilizer, gasoline for transport, etc.) to produce 1 ton of corn in the United States. As the cost of a barrel of oil has skyrocketed, so too has the price of grain. Economic models suggest that for every $1 rise in the price of a barrel of oil, U.S. grain prices, which determine world prices, could rise by 20 cents a bushel.

The rising cost of energy imports has also forced some developing nations to choose between importing oil or grain. For the farmer, higher energy prices have driven up the price of fertilizer (which can account for a third of soybean production costs in Brazil), electricity for irrigation pumps, and the costs of transporting produce to market. Most damaging is the high cost of gasoline that has increased U.S. planting of corn for ethanol.

Whatever gains are made in food production, they risk being overwhelmed if energy costs continue to spiral out of control.

- Soil erosion. Worldwide, croplands the size of Indiana disappear every year, according to studies by David Pimentel, a professor emeritus of ecology at Cornell University. "Erosion is a slow and insidious process," he said. "It nickels and dimes you to death. Yet the problem, which is growing ever more critical, is being ignored because who gets excited about dirt?"

The cost is already apparent in South Asia and sub-Saharan Africa, where a combination of population growth and poor land management has led to a 40 percent decline in arable cropland per capita since 1960.

Better land-use practices require agriculture extension services. Yet such services are nonexistent in many parts of the world because their cost and complexity exceed government capabilities and because they have not been in commercial farmers' short-term interests. Moreover, the inexorable pressure to increase production may overwhelm even the most-well-meaning soil conservation programs.

- Water shortages. Irrigation accounts for about 40 percent of the value of agricultural production worldwide. But that production is often being bought with overdrafts at the water bank. In China, farmers take about 25 percent more water from underground aquifers than the rains replenish. In parts of northwest India, the overdraft rate is 56 percent. No wonder the irrigated area per person around the world is shrinking by 1 percent per year. More-efficient irrigation methods do exist and are slowly being adopted. But farmers will also need expensive new varieties of staple crops that use less water.

- Climate change. This may be the gravest and most imponderable long-term challenge the food system faces. If temperatures increase moderately over the next half-century, agricultural production losses in tropical developing countries may be partially offset by production gains in temperate zones. But if temperatures rise by more than 3 degrees Celsius, an increasingly likely prospect scientists say, harvests could be severely affected everywhere, falling by a fifth in South Asia alone. The cost of adapting the food system to climate change could be tens of billions of dollars in developing countries alone, far exceeding available resources.

Long-Term, Not Stopgap

The current food crisis is a product of bad weather, higher energy costs, commodities speculation, and policy shifts that have had unintended consequences, notably U.S. ethanol subsidies and widespread export bans. It is also a harbinger of more-serious food challenges rooted in the inability of the food system to deal with market breakdowns, such as investment shortfalls in research and development and infrastructure, and with externalities, such as rising affluence and climate change.

Some of today's problems may eventually self-correct through a cyclical upturn in production and a downturn in prices. Tomorrow's food issues are more challenging.

"Food security will deteriorate further," Brown predicted, "unless leading countries can collectively mobilize to stabilize population, restrict the use of grain to produce automotive fuel, stabilize climate, stabilize water tables and aquifers, protect cropland, and conserve soils."

To accommodate this change, global institutions may need to be restructured to cope better with inevitable future agricultural market volatility.

"The IMF [International Monetary Fund] needs additional authority to provide bridge financing for countries faced with sharply rising food import bills," said Gus Schumacher, a former U.S. undersecretary of Agriculture. "It needs power to oversee hedge funds spiking commodity prices and to discourage food embargoes by wheat and rice exporters. And there needs to be some insurance facility to protect importing and exporting countries when drought and storms disrupt food supplies."

World leaders will review the food situation at the G-8 summit in July and at a United Nations food conference in September [2008]. The danger is that food prices may be receding by then and leaders, distracted by some new crisis, will be tempted to pursue stopgap measures instead of long-term solutions.

Government Policies Have Caused the Current Food Crisis

Dominic Lawson

British journalist Dominic Lawson is an editorial and opinion writer for The Independent.

Sometimes an entire philosophy can be glimpsed in a single remark. So I am grateful to Andrew Dorward of London's School of Oriental and African Studies for his explanation of why it would not be in the interests of Africans to adopt genetically modified herbicide-resistant crops. Dr Dorward told the *Financial Times* that this would be "disastrous for many poor households" because such crops would "allow the replacement of hand-weeding, which is a big source of income for many".

This is the sort of argument which would have dismissed the invention of the printing press as endangering the livelihood of monks and quill manufacturers. The monks, at least, were not engaged in back-breaking labour—unlike the sub-Saharan subsistence farmer, who under the blazing sun might spend up to 120 days weeding a single field, instead of utilising the time saved in cultivating new crops or tilling new fields. Yet this is the sort of grinding, life-shortening labour in which the advocates of so-called "sustainable development" wish to keep Africans enslaved—the sort of life which no Westerner would tolerate for himself or his family.

Liberalization of Markets

It is characteristic of the double standards which the international aid establishment has been promulgating for years— and which has been evident during the Rome food summit over the past few days [June 2008]. Thus John Hilary, of War on Want, claimed both that it was the "liberalisation" of agricultural markets which lay behind the international food crisis, and also that the Western world should end its protectionist farming policies.

He's right that we should do so—yet for some reason he will not utter a word of criticism against the much-higher agricultural tariffs that exist between the countries of sub-Saharan Africa, and which have an obvious and immediate role in making food more expensive for some of the poorest people on earth. Import controls in the developing world are a dramatic contributor to "food poverty"—so why is "market liberalisation" such a terrible idea?

Such impoverishing beggar-my-neighbour policies are defended by the likes of War on Want on the grounds that such actions by governments in the developing world are a proper exercise of "food sovereignty". In practice this actually means nothing more than the right of landowners—who tend to be government ministers—to extort monopoly rents at the expense of those less fortunate.

If I were a cynical man, I would wonder whether the international aid agencies had a vested interest in maintaining such a failed political and economic system, since it keeps entire populations in the state of dependence which justifies their own existence, and their regular appeals to our charitable conscience.

Government, Politicians, and Subsidies

Nevertheless, it is America which has once again been subject to the biggest criticism at an international summit—this time for its policy of vast ethanol subsidies, with its effect of turning about a quarter of what was its corn production into fuel for cars. Well, it is indeed absolutely indefensible—but if anyone thinks a President Barack Obama would change this policy, they would be very much mistaken. The Democrat candidate voiced his support for this grotesque subsidy on the campaign trail.

Although the ethanol racket was invented by George [W.] Bush when he realised that the Iraq war had failed in its second-order objective of increasing the supply of "friendly" oil from the Middle East, the 43rd US President is actually less keen on agricultural subsidies than the supposedly more enlightened Democrats.

[In May 2008] the Democrat-controlled Senate voted to extend and expand various US farm subsidies with a bill which it is estimated will cost American taxpayers $290bn [billion]. George Bush urged legislators to reject the bill and said he would veto it, if he could. Bush insisted that it would not just be an unconscionable hand-out to some of the country's biggest and richest landowners—at the expense of all taxpayers—but would also damage America's trade relationships.

You might argue that as an outgoing president with no need or opportunity to win a general election, George Bush could now afford to take a more high-minded approach. So note this: John McCain also declared that he would veto such a bill, were he to be elected president. And Barack Obama? He supported the bill. The head of Oxfam America, Ray Offenheiser, argued furiously that the $290bn subsidy bill would "hurt the world's poorest farmers". Perhaps Mr Offenheiser should ask Barack Obama to spare a thought—even in this election year—for his paternal relatives in Kenya.

The Common Agricultural Policy

Not, of course, that we in the European Union have the slightest reason to feel morally superior. The Common Agricultural Policy remains the most organised conspiracy to maintain global food prices at an artificially high level.

Douglas Alexander, the British Government's Secretary for International Development, was quite right to tell the Rome

food summit: "It is unacceptable that the rich countries still
subsidise farming by $1bn a day, costing poor farmers in de-
veloping countries an estimated $100bn a year in lost in-
come." It would have been even better if he had mentioned
the Common Agricultural Policy, specifically, in that statement.

---

*Across the world, almost every distortion of food produc-
tion, every misallocation of resources, can be attributed
to the interventions of governments.*

More to the point, I wonder why Gordon Brown—who
... sought to blame the Organisation of Petroleum Exporting
Countries (OPEC) for the high cost of petrol and diesel in
our filling stations—has not attacked the much more single-
minded cartel known as the Common Agricultural Policy for
its contribution to the cost of food in Britain's high streets.
Oh, I remember why, now: our country is a member of that
infamous cartel.

This is in part why I query the remarks by the Foreign Office minister, Lord Malloch-Brown, after Robert Mugabe had
dropped in to make a speech to the gathering. Malloch-Brown
declared that "Zimbabwe is one of the few countries whose
food crisis is not due to climate change or global prices, but
due to disastrous policies".

It's true that Zimbabwe is an extreme case, in which corrupt government policies of land requisition have turned the
former African "bread-basket" into a basket-case. Yet across
the world, almost every distortion of food production, every
misallocation of resources, can be attributed to the interventions of governments, whether as extorters of tax on food, or
as lackeys of landowners—or a bizarre combination of both.

In other words, it's not the unfettered free market and globalisation which has caused the world food crisis, but governments who insist that markets can not be trusted—unlike

them, of course. What is truly terrifying is that they continue, decade after decade, to get away with it.

Markets Can Bring Stability and Resolve the Current Food Crisis

Martin Wolf

Martin Wolf is associate editor and chief economics commentator for London's Financial Times. *His published books include* Why Globalization Works *and* Fixing Global Finance.

Of the two crises disturbing the world economy—financial disarray and soaring food prices—the latter is the more disturbing. In many developing countries, the poorest quartile of consumers spends close to three-quarters of its income on food. Inevitably, high prices threaten unrest at best and mass starvation at worst.

The recent price spikes apply to almost all significant food and feedstuffs. Yet these jumps are themselves part of a wider range of commodity price rises. Powerful forces are linking prices of energy, industrial raw materials and foodstuffs. Those forces include rapid economic growth in the emerging world, strains on world energy supplies, the weakness of the US dollar and global inflationary pressures.

Yet the food element of this story carries its own significance. . . . With rice and wheat prices spiking, riots on the streets of the Philippines, Egypt and Haiti and moves by India, Vietnam, Cambodia and China to restrict rice exports, food is suddenly an even hotter issue than normal.

So why have prices of food risen so strongly? Will these higher prices last? What action should be taken in response?

Why Prices of Food Have Risen So Sharply

On the demand side, strong rises in incomes per head in China, India and other emerging countries have raised demand for food, notably meat and the related animal feeds. These shifts in land use reduce the supply of cereals available for human consumption.

Furthermore, rising production of subsidised biofuels, further stimulated by soaring oil prices, boosts demand for maize, rapeseed oil and the other grains and edible oils that are an alternative to food crops. The latest World Economic Outlook from the International Monetary Fund comments that "although biofuels still account for only 1 1/2 per cent of the global liquid fuels supply, they accounted for almost half of the increase in consumption of major food crops in 2006–2007, mostly because of corn-based ethanol produced in the US".

Meanwhile, aggregate production of maize, rice and soyabeans stagnated in 2006 and 2007. This was partly the result of drought. Also important, however, have been higher prices of oil, since modern farming is so energy-intensive. With weak growth of supply and strong increases in demand, cereal stocks have fallen to their lowest levels since the early 1980s. Declining stocks undermine the widely shared belief that speculation has driven the rising prices, since stocks would be rising, not falling, if prices were above market-clearing levels.

Vastly more worrying than speculation is the weak medium-term growth of supply. The rapid increases in yields of the 1970s and 1980s, at the time of the "green revolution", have slowed. Given the stresses on water supplies, longer-term supply prospects would look poor even if diversion of land for production of biofuels were not adding to the pressure.

Bringing Down Food Prices

Are prices going to remain high? Two opposing forces are at work. The first is the market, which will tend to bring prices back down as supplies expand and demand shrinks. But the latter is also what we want to avoid, at least in the case of the poor, since reducing their consumption is not so much a solution as a failure. The second force is the current intense pressure on the world's food system. This is true of both demand and costs of supply. Prices are likely to remain relatively elevated, by historical standards, unless (or until) energy prices tumble.

This, then, brings us to the big question: what is to be done? The answers fall into three broad categories: humanitarian; trade and other policy interventions; and longer-term productivity and production.

The important point on the first is that higher food prices have powerful distributional effects: they hurt the poorest the most. This is true both among countries and within them. The Food and Agricultural Organisation in Rome [in June 2008] listed 37 countries in substantial need of food assistance. Moreover, according to the World Bank, soaring food prices threaten to make at least 100 [million] more people hungry.

The present crisis is a golden opportunity to eliminate . . . damaging [government] interventions.

Increases in aid to the vulnerable, either as food or as cash, are vital. Equally important, however, is ensuring that the additional supplies reach those in greatest difficulty. The options depend on the sophistication of a country's bureaucratic machinery. But they include work paid directly with food (which is a good way of screening out the better-off), a rationed supply of cheap food for the poor or cash vouchers. Those most in need will be the landless, both rural and urban, and marginal subsistence farmers.

Now turn to the policy interventions. Protection, subsidies and other such follies distort agriculture more than any other sector. Alas, the opportunity to eliminate protection against imports offered by exceptionally high world prices is not being taken. A host of countries are imposing export taxes instead, thereby fragmenting the world market still more, reducing incentives for increased output and penalising poor net-importing countries. Meanwhile, rich countries are encouraging, or even forcing, their farmers to grow fuel instead of food.

The present crisis is a golden opportunity to eliminate this plethora of damaging interventions. The political focus of the [World Trade Organization's] Doha round on lowering high levels of protection is largely irrelevant. The focus should, instead, be on shifting the farm sector towards the market, while cushioning the impact of high prices on the poor.

Finally, far greater resources need to be devoted to expanding long-run supply. Increased spending on research will be essential, especially into farming in dry-land conditions. The move towards genetically modified food in developing countries is as inevitable as that of the high-income countries towards nuclear power. At least as important will be more efficient use of water, via pricing and additional investment. People will oppose some of these policies. But mass starvation is not a tolerable option.

The food and fuel crisis of 2008 is a cry for our attention. Nobody knows how long these shocks will last. But they demand rapid policy changes across the globe. We must choose between fragmenting world markets still further and integrating them, between helping the poor and letting even more starve and between investing in improving supply and allowing food deficiencies to grow. The right choices are evident. The time to make them is now.

The Free Market Promotes Food Efficiency and Security

Bright B. Simons and Franklin Cudjoe

Bright B. Simons and Franklin Cudjoe are director of development and executive director, respectively, of the libertarian think tank IMANI: Centre for Education & Policy.

Recently, a commentator published an article about the free market and food security on a much patronised Ghanaian news website. Full of passion, but, unfortunately, lacking in depth of analysis, his views summarises a great deal of the reactions to the so-called global food crisis that have come from leftist or left of center pundits in recent weeks. We are taking the opportunity therefore to use excerpts of his article to address many of the left-leaning misconceptions that have characterised the debate so far.

In said article the writer, one [Kwami] Agbodza, accuses the free market of many crimes, though he takes pains to prove none of them. He acknowledges that the reasons advanced for the general rise in food price levels are numerous and complex, but offers in the same breath a point of view that suggests that free-market driven, private sector based policies are solely responsible for the supposed crisis. To crown this string of insights, he asserts, without evidence or argument, that "However, the free market private sector has little interest in feeding Ghana by meeting the costs of this required investment."

The facts of the matter, as far as the food security issue is concerned, are in direct contradiction of most of Mr. Agbodza's claims. We will examine his key assertions one after the other.

The Free Market and Biofuels Production

"You have land-producing food and you switch it to produce biofuel when you cannot feed yourself; who in their right mind will do this except the lunatic free market."

The free market or its proponents have never been the driving force behind the fashionable trend towards farmland conversion to biofuel use. Indeed, by freemarket terms, biofuel production was unprofitable, and therefore unadvised, until very recently. The steam that pushed farmers to switch to biofuel production in certain countries was supplied by government and foundation subsidies under the well-intentioned, but misguided, belief that biofuels could replace less environmentally friendly fossil fuels. The most enthusiastic national producers of biofuel, on GDP [gross domestic product] relativity terms, were countries like Malaysia and Brazil. None of these countries can be accused of a history of being pushed around by free market fundamentalists. More often than not, centrally devised "national development plans" made biofuel exploitation a cardinal feature of economic policy. The Brazilian project Mr. Agbodza cites has been brought to Ghana under the auspices of the unquestionably leftist Lula Da Silva, President of Brazil, not libertarian activists in Rio.

Mr. Agbodza makes the elementary error that free market ideology is identical to "corporatism", which one will suppose equates to a belief that "syndicalism" is the same thing as scientific Marxism. Rule by giant corporations has been seen under both fascist and communist regimes, but is abhorred by all classical liberals. Corporations are not natural allies of free market enthusiasts. In fact for each group of shareholders of corporation X, the best market conditions might actually be found in the situation where corporation X enjoys a monopoly in the industry granted by a corrupt government. Classical liberal free market ideology is about "competition, competition, competition". The central tenets of the libertarian faith, such as comparative advantage and property rights, are all glued together by the principle of just, free, and unfettered competition amongst enterprises to service the self-determined needs of free individuals on a level playing field guaranteed by impartial institutions. We sincerely doubt that Mr. Agbodza, when he refers to the free market, actually understand the matter at hand to adequate depth.

The Error of the "Imports Bad, Exports Good" Cry

"What we know for a fact for Ghana is that like all other developing countries we now have to spend a lot more on food imports. There are estimates developing countries spend up to 80% of their budget on food imports."

The point Mr. Agbodza wants to make with the statement above is not clear, but it appears he is rehashing the old theme: "imports bad, exports good". Once upon a time, that viewpoint would have been laughed out of court as "mercantilism". Why do we have to spend "more" for food imports? For as long as I can remember the concern of leftist-statists like Mr. Agbodza had been that we were the victims of price-dumping. As a result of the Common Agricultural Policy, they argued, we, here in Africa, were being inundated with cheap food. Now that a temporary blip in food prices is being observed, the argument has taken a 180° turn: we are being hammered with expensive food. The resolution of this false puzzle is a matter of basic economics.

If food imports were indeed expensive, local producers would simply have exercised their comparative advantage (akin to what some call market arbitrage) and begun to recapture market from importers. If there is a genuine case of alarmingly increasing food imports (an odd scenario giving that malnutrition is supposedly still a concern, and we are yet to see surplus imported food being carted into the sea), the sound inference can only be that they are relatively cheap. If they are, then Ghanaians are saving resources (by buying relatively cheap food) that can be used in other economic endeavours. If a trend is discovered that suggest categories of food that used to be produced in Ghana are now being imported, then that trend should be seen as an economic signal highlighting Ghana's growing uncompetitiveness across those relevant categories. Those signals are then used by shrewd local investors to shift resources around to areas where Ghanaian production factors suggest greater competitiveness. Jobs lost in the old uncompetitive economic sectors are re-gained by new jobs being created in the competitive economic sectors. A decline in public sector productivity led to retrenchment across the civil service while an improvement in the macroeconomic indicators gingered growth in the banking sector. The consequence so far has been that newly minted gems from the University of Ghana Business School troop to the banking halls of Ring Road Central rather than to the HR [Human Resources] department of Cocobod.

Efficient use in the medium term benefits the society at large because scarce resources are put to the most rewarding use.

To return to the issue of food security, if readers will allow us. Considering that somewhere between 60% and 65% of Ghanaians are engaged in the agricultural sector, whereas in most developed countries the corresponding percentage is lower than 5%, one clearly sees the argument that this amounts to underutilized human resources. The critical issue therefore is that the sector can do with greater efficiency. The cry over rural folk departing to urban centers is misplaced if not positioned within the broader context of efficiency. Basic economics means that the more peasant-style farmers leave the rural areas, the more land is freed. The lower agricultural land is priced (note that there could also be a transfer of "unproductive" agricultural land to more productive use such as, perhaps, tourism) and the more attractive commercial farming becomes. Mr. Agbodza breezily dismissed such arguments as harking to a tired old free market theme of "equilibrium". We will not use that term. We prefer "efficiency". Efficiency means that resources will go to those areas that will best generate economic outcomes that reduce poverty by creating newer, better-paying jobs, and wealth for entrepreneurs most likely to re-invest (rather than old, competition-hating elites who probably fancy the Kensington homes Mr. Agbodza rails about).

The Free Market vs. Experts

"The private sector will only be interested in solving our food problem if there is higher normal or supernormal profit compared to other avenues and food (rice) imports."

In the free market, truly free, competitive system, the entrepreneur will put his/her money where he/she can make the most efficient use of it. Efficient use in the medium term benefits the society at large because scarce resources are put to the most rewarding use. Not where the personal biases of Mr. Agbodza determine.

"The costs of solving our rice (and food) import problem will include long-term (50–100 years) strategic planning, development of irrigation systems, funding agricultural research institutions, development of pragmatic and goal-oriented agricultural practices and a deep interest in citizens of Ghana."

A lot of long phrases, but the sentiment is clear enough. In the absence of a pro-forma national budget that will determine the sources of funding for the initiatives listed above (assuming of course that those areas have been neglected and are being neglected in Ghana) and the opportunity costs for implementing these as opposed to building, say, more vocational schools, one can hardly debate the merits of such suggestions. We can attack it on principle though. A hundred year plan is misguided. Mr Agbodza proves by this suggestion that he is a consummate statist, central plan loving techno-crat. Sadly the pace of technological change and the turbu-lence of politics and socio-economic transformation means that even were you to assemble all Nobel Laureates, dead and alive, in all fields, to this task, you are [more] likely to get it wrong than right. Knowledge is simply too scarce to be treated so inefficiently. As justification for our position, consider that, of the many pundits in the mid-century futurism industry, none predicted the growth of the internet. Then consider how the online distribution model has reshaped global economics. The typical leftist position of: "let the experts tell us all how to live" has proved damaging to economic growth wherever it has been tried.

The problem in Ghana and Africa is not an excess of free market enthusiasm, but a dearth of it.

"*Until a country such as Ghana is sufficient in food produc-tion, scarce agricultural land should never be used for the pro-duction of non-food crops.*"

As arguments against free markets go, Mr. Agbodza's usu-ally tend to belong to the category that was in fashion 2 de-cades ago. Self-sufficiency in the production of any good or service of national importance can not be a virtue in and of itself. Even the most vociferous statists concede that trade has a part to play in the self-sufficiency quest. Otherwise, why, one might as well argue for self-sufficiency at the homestead level. After all, one does not know when an apocalyptic eruption will force us all to lock our doors behind us and bunker in for years on end. Operation feed yourself, then! The truth though is that in places like Hong Kong, Singapore, and increasingly the Middle East, trade has proved sufficient in allowing citi-zens to maintain sound food security. Who is to determine what "scarce" agricultural land is? Mr. Agbodza? Another com-mittee of experts paid with World Bank money? The free market has proved more skilled and farsighted in determining when land is scarce and when it is plentiful than any assembly of experts ever convened by any standing committee of any centralized state.

Anti-Free Market Arguments
vs. The Evidence

"This is the anti-free market food policy that will ensure our strategic food security. If implemented, it will be sound economic governance."

But tons of data and mountains of evidence disprove that claim. According to reports produced by the UNDP [United Nations Development Programme] (definitely not a bastion of free market economics) between 1997 and 2003, world poverty has fallen more in the past 50 years than it did during the preceding 500. In just under thirty years, poverty in Asia has fallen from 60% of the population to less than 20% today [2008]. According to the FAO [Food and Agriculture Organization] (also not a bastion of the free market), malnourishment in the developing world has declined from nearly 40% to less than 20% today (even with significant population growth) in the past 30 years. Since 1980, food prices have dropped by more than 30% even after accommodating recent price rises. The green revolution has seen grain production increase by almost 50% across the developing world. There isn't a single shred of evidence that those parts of the world that have gained the most have done so by progressively centralizing the state and undermining free markets. Indeed, throughout Asia, the contrary is true. Even Maoist China is deregulating its land tenure system. Nor is there any proof, whatsoever, that African countries, that have gained the least, have suffered as a result of a historic tendency to liberate their markets. Indeed, again, the contrary is true. It is barely two decades that Ghana begun its market reform program, and even then only grudgingly and at the instance of external forces.

As Mr. Agbodza has so blatantly shown, the problem in Ghana and Africa is not an excess of free market enthusiasm, but a dearth of it, particularly amongst the intellectual classes. We dare hope that this is a situation that will change rapidly, else another wave of global progress will pass us by, once again.

Current Controversies

Chapter 2

Is the Demand for Biofuels Fueling the Global Food Crisis?

Chapter Preface

In the 1970s and 1980s, with oil prices rising and domestic production in decline, the United States began to look for alternate sources of fuel. Biofuels had been widely used to power cars in the early part of the century, but after the 1930s they had been supplanted by petroleum, thanks to the efforts of powerful "oil barons" with a vested interest in promoting the use of their product. With the mass production of cars and the development of an economy built on inexpensive petroleum, American need soon outstripped domestic production, and by the 1970s Americans were almost completely dependent on foreign sources of oil. The Middle East oil embargo in 1973 prompted researchers to once again investigate the use of vegetable and plant oils to begin reducing the country's dependence on foreign oil and be able to meet increasingly stringent environmental standards. In 1988, corn-derived ethanol was added to gasoline for the purpose of reducing carbon monoxide emissions. After a surge in gas prices after 2001, environmentally conscious consumers began switching over to cars powered by biodiesel in the belief that the alternative vegetable-based fuel was cleaner, greener, and the solution to everything from global warming to expensive and unjust wars.

The growing appeal of biodiesel led to increased production in the 2000s, and in December 2007, then-President George W. Bush signed into law the "Energy Independence and Security Act" mandating that the United States produce 36 billion gallons of biofuels every year by 2022, an almost fivefold increase over 2006 production levels. The energy policy was warmly embraced by representatives and constituents in corn-growing states, and on the presidential campaign trail Barack Obama touted the importance of ethanol to American's energy security. However, questions over the viability of biofuels as an energy source began to emerge, and with the sudden increase in grain prices in 2007, people began to take a critical view of the use of food to create fuel.

Biodiesel went quickly from a "green" energy source to a source of controversy, as critics claimed that the diversion of food crops to produce fuel was immoral. While people in the Third World were starving, fumed many commentators in developing nations, Europeans and Americans were converting grain to fill up their vehicles, and driving up food prices in the process. The United Nations' special rapporteur, Jean Ziegler, went so far as to label biofuel production a "crime against humanity" and called for an end to production in the United States and European Union. The International Monetary Fund argued that biofuels have become an issue of ethics and that a moratorium is needed on their production. Many economists and scientists echoed these views as well, suggesting that the environmental impact of producing biodiesels was as bad as the use of fossil fuels. Using acreage to grow grains for biodiesel, according to some experts, would also boost the carbon dioxide emissions that cause global warming, which in turn would have devastating effects on agriculture and food security.

Supporters of biofuels have been quick to reject the idea that the production of an alternative, renewable fuel source has been the source of rising food prices worldwide. Ethanol producers argue that one of the largest factors in skyrocketing food prices was the high cost of oil, and biofuels are an economically viable alternative to combat the high price of petroleum required for food production and transportation. Brazil, the world's largest producer of sugarcane-based ethanol, has insisted that its production of crops for the fuel has positively impacted food production and had clear environmental benefits. Others have argued that it is not the production of biofuels *per se* but the protectionist policies of European and American governments and the massive subsidies given to biofuel farmers in powerful countries that have aggravated the crisis. In the face of this criticism, bioenergy has become a controversial topic, and plans for increasing available lands for biofuel production in Europe and the United States are being reviewed.

The Exorbitant Corn Requirements for Biofuels Have Created a Food Crisis

C. Ford Runge and Benjamin Senauer

C. Ford Runge is Distinguished McKnight University Professor of Applied Economics and Law and director of the Center for International Food and Agricultural Policy at the University of Minnesota. Benjamin Senauer is professor of Applied Economics and co-director of the Food Industry Center at the University of Minnesota.

In 1974, as the United States was reeling from the oil embargo imposed by the Organization of Petroleum Exporting Countries [OPEC], Congress took the first of many legislative steps to promote ethanol made from corn as an alternative fuel. On April 18, 1977, amid mounting calls for energy independence, President Jimmy Carter donned his cardigan sweater and appeared on television to tell Americans that balancing energy demands with available domestic resources would be an effort the "moral equivalent of war." The gradual phaseout of lead in the 1970s and 1980s provided an additional boost to the fledgling ethanol industry. (Lead, a toxic substance, is a performance enhancer when added to gasoline, and it was partly replaced by ethanol.) A series of tax breaks and subsidies also helped. In spite of these measures, with each passing year the United States became more dependent on imported petroleum, and ethanol remained marginal at best.

Now, thanks to a combination of high oil prices and even more generous government subsidies, corn-based ethanol has become the rage. There were 110 ethanol refineries in operation in the United States at the end of 2006, according to the

Renewable Fuels Association. Many were being expanded, and another 73 were under construction. When these projects are completed, by the end of 2008, the United States' ethanol production capacity will reach an estimated 11.4 billion gallons per year. In his latest State of the Union address, President George W. Bush called on the country to produce 35 billion gallons of renewable fuel a year by 2017, nearly five times the level currently mandated.

Ethanol and Taxpayer Subsidies

The push for ethanol and other biofuels has spawned an industry that depends on billions of dollars of taxpayer subsidies, and not only in the United States. In 2005, global ethanol production was 9.66 billion gallons, of which Brazil produced 45.2 percent (from sugar cane) and the United States 44.5 percent (from corn). Global production of biodiesel (most of it in Europe), made from oilseeds, was almost one billion gallons.

The industry's growth has meant that a larger and larger share of corn production is being used to feed the huge mills that produce ethanol. According to some estimates, ethanol plants will burn up to half of U.S. domestic corn supplies within a few years. Ethanol demand will bring 2007 inventories of corn to their lowest levels since 1995 (a drought year), even though 2006 yielded the third-largest corn crop on record. Iowa may soon become a net corn importer.

The enormous volume of corn required by the ethanol industry is sending shock waves through the food system. (The United States accounts for some 40 percent of the world's total corn production and over half of all corn exports.) In March 2007, corn futures rose to over $4.38 a bushel, the highest level in ten years. Wheat and rice prices have also surged to decade highs, because even as those grains are increasingly being used as substitutes for corn, farmers are planting more acres with corn and fewer acres with other crops.

This might sound like nirvana to corn producers, but it is hardly that for consumers, especially in poor developing countries, who will be hit with a double shock if both food prices and oil prices stay high. The World Bank has estimated that in 2001, 2.7 billion people in the world were living on the equivalent of less than $2 a day; to them, even marginal increases in the cost of staple grains could be devastating. Filling the 25-gallon tank of an SUV with pure ethanol requires over 450 pounds of corn—which contains enough calories to feed one person for a year. By putting pressure on global supplies of edible crops, the surge in ethanol production will translate into higher prices for both processed and staple foods around the world. Biofuels have tied oil and food prices together in ways that could profoundly upset the relationships between food producers, consumers, and nations in the years ahead, with potentially devastating implications for both global poverty and food security.

The Oil and Biofuel Economy

In the United States and other large economies, the ethanol industry is artificially buoyed by government subsidies, minimum production levels, and tax credits. High oil prices over the past few years have made ethanol naturally competitive, but the U.S. government continues to heavily subsidize corn farmers and ethanol producers. Direct corn subsidies equaled $8.9 billion in 2005. Although these payments will fall in 2006 and 2007 because of high corn prices, they may soon be dwarfed by the panoply of tax credits, grants, and government loans included in energy legislation passed in 2005 and in a pending farm bill designed to support ethanol producers. The federal government already grants ethanol blenders a tax allowance of 51 cents per gallon of ethanol they make, and many states pay out additional subsidies.

Consumption of ethanol in the United States was expected to reach over 6 billion gallons in 2006. (Consumption of biodiesel was expected to be about 250 million gallons.) In 2005, the U.S. government mandated the use of 7.5 billion gallons of biofuels per year by 2012; in early 2007, 37 governors proposed raising that figure to 12 billion gallons by 2010; and ... President Bush raised it further, to 35 billion gallons by 2017. Six billion gallons of ethanol are needed every year to replace the fuel additive known as MTBE, which is being phased out due to its polluting effects on ground water.

The European Commission is using legislative measures and directives to promote biodiesel, produced mainly in Europe, made from rapeseeds and sunflower seeds. In 2005, the European Union [EU] produced 890 million gallons of biodiesel, over 80 percent of the world's total. The EU's Common Agricultural Policy also promotes the production of ethanol from a combination of sugar beets and wheat with direct and indirect subsidies. Brussels aims to have 5.75 percent of motor fuel consumed in the European Union come from biofuels by 2010 and 10 percent by 2020.

As more acres are planted with corn, land will have to be pulled from other crops or environmentally fragile areas.

Brazil, which currently produces approximately the same amount of ethanol as the United States, derives almost all of it from sugar cane. Like the United States, Brazil began its quest for alternative energy in the mid-1970s. The government has offered incentives, set technical standards, and invested in supporting technologies and market promotion. It has mandated that all diesel contain two percent biodiesel by 2008 and five percent biodiesel by 2013. It has also required that the auto industry produce engines that can use biofuels and has developed wide-ranging industrial and land-use strategies to promote them. Other countries are also jumping on the biofuel bandwagon. In Southeast Asia, vast areas of tropical forest are being cleared and burned to plant oil palms destined for conversion to biodiesel.

This trend has strong momentum. Despite a recent decline, many experts expect the price of crude oil to remain high in the long term. Demand for petroleum continues to increase faster than supplies, and new sources of oil are often expensive to exploit or located in politically risky areas. According to the U.S. Energy Information Administration's latest projections, global energy consumption will rise by 71 percent between 2003 and 2030, with demand from developing countries, notably China and India, surpassing that from members of the Organization for Economic Cooperation and Development by 2015. The result will be sustained upward pressure on oil prices, which will allow ethanol and biodiesel producers to pay much higher premiums for corn and oilseeds than was conceivable just a few years ago. The higher oil prices go, the higher ethanol prices can go while remaining competitive—and the more ethanol producers can pay for corn. If oil reaches $80 per barrel, ethanol producers could afford to pay well over $5 per bushel for corn.

Price Increases in All Agricultural Sectors

With the price of raw materials at such highs, the biofuel craze would place significant stress on other parts of the agricultural sector. In fact, it already does. In the United States, the growth of the biofuel industry has triggered increases not only in the prices of corn, oilseeds, and other grains but also in the prices of seemingly unrelated crops and products. The use of land to grow corn to feed the ethanol maw is reducing the acreage devoted to other crops. Food processors who use crops such as peas and sweet corn have been forced to pay higher prices to keep their supplies secure—costs that will eventually be passed on to consumers. Rising feed prices are also hitting the livestock and poultry industries. According to

Vernon Eidman, a professor emeritus of agribusiness management at the University of Minnesota, higher feed costs have caused returns to fall sharply, especially in the poultry and swine sectors. If returns continue to drop, production will decline, and the prices for chicken, turkey, pork, milk, and eggs will rise. A number of Iowa's pork producers could go out of business in the next few years as they are forced to compete with ethanol plants for corn supplies.

Proponents of corn-based ethanol argue that acreage and yields can be increased to satisfy the rising demand for ethanol. But U.S. corn yields have been rising by a little less than two percent annually over the last ten years, and even a doubling of those gains could not meet current demand. As more acres are planted with corn, land will have to be pulled from other crops or environmentally fragile areas, such as those protected by the Department of Agriculture's Conservation Reserve Program.

In addition to these fundamental forces, speculative pressures have created what might be called a "biofuel mania": prices are rising because many buyers think they will. Hedge funds are making huge bets on corn and the bull market unleashed by ethanol. The biofuel mania is commandeering grain stocks with a disregard for the obvious consequences. It seems to unite powerful forces, including motorists' enthusiasm for large, fuel-inefficient vehicles and guilt over the ecological consequences of petroleum-based fuels. But even as ethanol has created opportunities for huge profits for agribusiness, speculators, and some farmers, it has upset the traditional flows of commodities and the patterns of trade and consumption both inside and outside of the agricultural sector.

This craze will create a different problem if oil prices decline because of, say, a slowdown in the global economy. With oil at $30 a barrel, producing ethanol would no longer be profitable unless corn sold for less than $2 a bushel, and that would spell a return to the bad old days of low prices for U.S. farmers. Undercapitalized ethanol plants would be at risk, and farmer-owned cooperatives would be especially vulnerable. Calls for subsidies, mandates, and tax breaks would become even more shrill than they are now: there would be clamoring for a massive bailout of an overinvested industry. At that point, the major investments that have been made in biofuels would start to look like a failed gamble. On the other hand, if oil prices hover around $55–$60, ethanol producers could pay from $3.65 to $4.54 for a bushel of corn and manage to make a normal 12 percent profit.

Whatever happens in the oil market, the drive for energy independence, which has been the basic justification for huge investments in and subsidies for ethanol production, has already made the industry dependent on high oil prices.

The Politics of Corn

One root of the problem is that the biofuel industry has long been dominated not by market forces but by politics and the interests of a few large companies. Corn has become the prime raw material even though biofuels could be made efficiently from a variety of other sources, such as grasses and wood chips, if the government funded the necessary research and development. But in the United States, at least, corn and soybeans have been used as primary inputs for many years thanks in large part to the lobbying efforts of corn and soybean growers and Archer Daniels Midland Company (ADM), the biggest ethanol producer in the U.S. market.

Since the late 1960s, ADM positioned itself as the "supermarket to the world" and aimed to create value from bulk commodities by transforming them into processed products that command heftier prices. In the 1970s, ADM started making ethanol and other products resulting from the wet-milling of corn, such as high fructose corn syrup. It quickly grew from a minor player in the feed market to a global powerhouse. By 1980, ADM's ethanol production had reached 175 million gallons per year, and high fructose corn syrup had become a ubiquitous sweetening agent in processed foods. In 2006, ADM was the largest producer of ethanol in the United States: it made more than 1.07 billion gallons, over four times more than its nearest rival, VeraSun Energy. In early 2006, it announced plans to increase its capital investment in ethanol from $700 million to $1.2 billion in 2008 and increase production by 47 percent, or close to 500 million gallons, by 2009.

ADM owes much of its growth to political connections, especially to key legislators who can earmark special subsidies for its products. Vice President Hubert Humphrey advanced many such measures when he served as a senator from Minnesota. Senator Bob Dole (R-Kans.) advocated tirelessly for the company during his long career. As the conservative critic James Bovard noted over a decade ago, nearly half of ADM's profits have come from products that the U.S. government has either subsidized or protected.

The ethanol industry has . . . become a theater of protectionism in U.S. trade policy.

Partly as a result of such government support, ethanol (and to a lesser extent biodiesel) is now a major fixture of the United States' agricultural and energy sectors. In addition to the federal government's 51-cents-per-gallon tax credit for ethanol, smaller producers get a 10-cents-per-gallon tax reduction on the first 15 million gallons they produce. There is also the "renewable fuel standard," a mandatory level of non-fossil fuel to be used in motor vehicles, which has set off a political bidding war. Despite already high government subsidies, Congress is considering lavishing more money on biofuels. Legislation related to the 2007 farm bill introduced by Representative Ron Kind (D-Wis.) calls for raising loan guarantees for ethanol producers from $200 million to $2 billion. Advocates of corn-based ethanol have rationalized subsidies by pointing out that greater ethanol demand pushes up corn prices and brings down subsidies to corn growers.

The ethanol industry has also become a theater of protectionism in U.S. trade policy. Unlike oil imports, which come into the country duty-free, most ethanol currently imported into the United States carries a 54-cents-per-gallon tariff, partly because cheaper ethanol from countries such as Brazil threatens U.S. producers. (Brazilian sugar cane can be converted to ethanol more efficiently than can U.S. corn.) The Caribbean Basin Initiative [CBI] could undermine this protection: Brazilian ethanol can already be shipped duty-free to CBI countries, such as Costa Rica, El Salvador, or Jamaica, and the agreement allows it to go duty-free from there to the United States. But ethanol supporters in Congress are pushing for additional legislation to limit those imports. Such government measures shield the industry from competition despite the damaging repercussions for consumers.

Starving the Hungry

Biofuels may have even more devastating effects in the rest of the world, especially on the prices of basic foods. If oil prices remain high—which is likely—the people most vulnerable to the price hikes brought on by the biofuel boom will be those in countries that both suffer food deficits and import petroleum. The risk extends to a large part of the developing world: in 2005, according to the UN [United Nations] Food and Agriculture Organization, most of the 82 low-income countries with food deficits were also net oil importers.

Even major oil exporters that use their petrodollars to purchase food imports, such as Mexico, cannot escape the consequences of the hikes in food prices. In late 2006, the price of tortilla flour in Mexico, which gets 80 percent of its corn imports from the United States, doubled thanks partly to a rise in U.S. corn prices from $2.80 to $4.20 a bushel over the previous several months. (Prices rose even though tortillas are made mainly from Mexican-grown white corn because industrial users of the imported yellow corn, which is used for animal feed and processed foods, started buying the cheaper white variety.) The price surge was exacerbated by speculation and hoarding. With about half of Mexico's 107 million people living in poverty and relying on tortillas as a main source of calories, the public outcry was fierce. In January 2007, Mexico's new president, Felipe Calderón, was forced to cap the prices of corn products.

The history of industrial demand for agricultural crops ... suggests that large producers [not peasant farmers] will be the main beneficiaries [of ethanol production from cassava].

The International Food Policy Research Institute, in Washington, D.C., has produced sobering estimates of the potential global impact of the rising demand for biofuels. Mark Rosegrant, an IFPRI [International Food Policy Research Institute] division director, and his colleagues project that given continued high oil prices, the rapid increase in global biofuel production will push global corn prices up by 20 percent by 2010 and 41 percent by 2020. The prices of oilseeds, including soybeans, rapeseeds, and sunflower seeds, are projected to rise by 26 percent by 2010 and 76 percent by 2020, and wheat prices by 11 percent by 2010 and 30 percent by 2020. In the poorest parts of sub-Saharan Africa, Asia, and Latin America, where cassava is a staple, its price is expected to increase by 33 percent by 2010 and 135 percent by 2020. The projected price increases may be mitigated if crop yields increase substantially or ethanol production based on other raw materials (such as trees and grasses) becomes commercially viable. But unless biofuel policies change significantly, neither development is likely.

The Future of Cassava-Based Fuel

The production of cassava-based ethanol may pose an especially grave threat to the food security of the world's poor. Cassava, a tropical potato-like tuber also known as manioc, provides one-third of the caloric needs of the population in sub-Saharan Africa and is the primary staple for over 200 million of Africa's poorest people. In many tropical countries, it is the food people turn to when they cannot afford anything else. It also serves as an important reserve when other crops fail because it can grow in poor soils and dry conditions and can be left in the ground to be harvested as needed.

Thanks to its high-starch content, cassava is also an excellent source of ethanol. As the technology for converting it to fuel improves, many countries—including China, Nigeria, and Thailand—are considering using more of the crop to that end. If peasant farmers in developing countries could become suppliers for the emerging industry, they would benefit from the increased income. But the history of industrial demand for agricultural crops in these countries suggests that large producers will be the main beneficiaries. The likely result of a boom in cassava-based ethanol production is that an increasing number of poor people will struggle even more to feed themselves.

Participants in the 1996 World Food Summit set out to cut the number of chronically hungry people in the world—people who do not eat enough calories regularly to be healthy and active—from 823 million in 1990 to about 400 million by 2015. The Millennium Development Goals established by the United Nations in 2000 vowed to halve the proportion of the world's chronically underfed population from 16 percent in 1990 to eight percent in 2015. Realistically, however, resorting to biofuels is likely to exacerbate world hunger. Several studies by economists at the World Bank and elsewhere suggest that caloric consumption among the world's poor declines by about half of one percent whenever the average prices of all major food staples increase by one percent. When one staple becomes more expensive, people try to replace it with a cheaper one, but if the prices of nearly all staples go up, they are left with no alternative.

In a study of global food security we conducted in 2003, we projected that given the rates of economic and population growth, the number of hungry people throughout the world would decline by 23 percent, to about 625 million, by 2025, so long as agricultural productivity improved enough to keep the relative price of food constant. But if, all other things being equal, the prices of staple foods increased because of demand for biofuels, as the IFPRI projections suggest they will, the number of food-insecure people in the world would rise by over 16 million for every percentage increase in the real prices of staple foods. That means that 1.2 billion people could be chronically hungry by 2025—600 million more than previously predicted.

The world's poorest people already spend 50 to 80 percent of their total household income on food. For the many among them who are landless laborers or rural subsistence farmers, large increases in the prices of staple foods will mean malnutrition and hunger. Some of them will tumble over the edge of subsistence into outright starvation, and many more will die from a multitude of hunger-related diseases.

The Policies that Favor Biofuels Have Created Food Shortages

Ronald Bailey

Ronald Bailey is Reason *magazine's science correspondent and author of the book* Liberation Biology: The Scientific and Moral Case for the Biotech Revolution.

[B]etween April 2007 and April 2008], the price of wheat has tripled, corn doubled, and rice almost doubled. As prices soared, food riots have broken out in about 20 poor countries including Yemen, Haiti, Egypt, Pakistan, Indonesian, Ivory Coast, and Mexico. In response some countries, such as India, Pakistan, Egypt and Vietnam, are banning the export of grains and imposing food price controls.

Are rising food prices the result of the economic dynamism of China and India, in which newly prosperous consumers are demanding more food—especially more meat? Perennial doomsters such as the Earth Policy Institute's Lester Brown predicted more than a decade ago that China's growing food demand would destabilize global markets and signal a permanent increase in grain prices. But that thesis has so far not been borne out by the facts. China is a net grain exporter. India is also largely self-sufficient in grains. At some time in the future, these countries may become net grain importers, but they are not now and so cannot be blamed for today's higher food prices.

The Culprit: Mistaken Energy Policies

If surging demand is not the problem, what is? In three words: Stupid energy policies. Although they are not perfect substitutes, oil and natural gas prices tend to move in tandem. So as oil prices rose above $100 per barrel, the price of gas also went up. Natural gas is the main feedstock for nitrogen fertilizer. As gas prices soared, so did fertilizer prices which rose by 200 percent.

As a report from the International Center for Soil Fertility and Agricultural Development (ICSFAD) notes, applying the fertilizer derived from 1000 cubic feet of natural gas yields around 480 pounds of grain. That amount of grain would supply enough calories to feed a person for one year. Rising oil prices also contribute to higher food prices because farmers need transport fuel to run their tractors and to get food to urban markets.

Even worse is the bioethanol craze. Politicians in both the United States and the European Union are mandating that vast quantities of food be turned into fuel as they chase the chimera of "energy independence." For example, Congress passed and President George W. Bush signed misbegotten legislation requiring fuel producers to use at least 36 billion gallons of biofuels by 2022—which equals about 27 percent of the gasoline Americans currently use each year and is about five times the amount being produced now. And the European Union set a goal that 10 percent of transport fuels come from biofuels by 2020.

Expanding acreage to grow biofuels is bad for biodiversity and may even boost the carbon dioxide emissions that contribute to man-made global warming.

The result of these mandates is that about 100 million tons of grain will be transformed this year into fuel, drawing down global grain stocks to their lowest levels in decades. Keep in mind that 100 million tons of grain is enough to feed nearly 450 million people for a year.

The Impact of Corn-Based Ethanol on Other Commodities

As Dennis Avery from the Hudson Institute's Center for Global Food Issues points out, the higher corn prices that result from biofuels mandates mean that farmers are shifting from producing wheat and soybeans to producing corn. Less wheat and soybeans means higher prices for those grains. In the face of higher prices for wheat, corn and soybeans consumers try to shift to rice which in turns raises that grain's price. In addition, higher grain prices encourage farmers in developing countries to chop down and plow up forests. It also hasn't helped that some traditionally strong grain exporters such as Australia have experienced extreme weather.

So what to do? In the short run, there is some good news. High prices are encouraging farmers to shift back toward wheat and soybeans which should relieve some of the pressure on grain prices. Second, the biofuels mandates must go. If biofuels are such a good idea, entrepreneurs, inventors and investors will make them into a viable energy source without any government subsidies. Thirdly, both high and low technologies are addressing high fertilizer prices. On the high tech front, Arcadia Biosciences has created biotech rice and corn varieties that need much less nitrogen fertilizer than conventional varieties require. In Bangladesh and other poor countries, farmers are embedding low tech fertilizer-infused briquettes in the soil to deliver nitrogen to rice. This boosts crop production 25 percent while cutting fertilizer use by 50 percent.

Expanding acreage to grow biofuels is bad for biodiversity and may even boost the carbon dioxide emissions that contribute to man-made global warming. Avery notes that food production needs to double because there will be more people who will want to eat better by 2050, at which point world population begins to slide back downwards. Turning food into fuel makes that goal much harder to achieve. Avery is right when he argues, "Biofuels are purely and simply the biggest Green mistake we've ever made and we're still making it."

Biofuels Have Had the Biggest Impact on Rising Food Prices

Aditya Chakrabortty

Aditya Chakrabortty is an economics writer for The Guardian.

Biofuels have forced global food prices up by 75%—far more than previously estimated—according to a confidential World Bank report obtained by *The Guardian.*

The damning unpublished assessment is based on the most detailed analysis of the crisis so far, carried out by an internationally-respected economist at [the] global financial body.

The figure emphatically contradicts the US government's claims that plant-derived fuels contribute less than 3% to food-price rises. It will add to pressure on governments in Washington and across Europe, which have turned to plant-derived fuels to reduce emissions of greenhouse gases and reduce their dependence on imported oil.

Senior development sources believe the report, completed in April [2008], has not been published to avoid embarrassing President George [W.] Bush.

"It would put the World Bank in a political hot-spot with the White House," said one. . . .

International Discussions and Lobbyists

The news comes at critical point in the world's negotiations on biofuels policy. Leaders of the G8 [Group of 8] industrialised countries meet [in July 2008] in Hokkaido, Japan, where they will discuss the food crisis and come under intense lobbying from campaigners calling for a moratorium on the use of plant-derived fuels.

Aditya Chakrabortty, "Secret Report: Biofuel Caused Food Crisis," *The Guardian*, July 4, 2008. Copyright © 2008 Guardian Newspapers Limited. Reproduced by permission of Guardian News Service, LTD.

It will also put pressure on the British government, which is due to release its own report on the impact of biofuels, the Gallagher Report. *The Guardian* has previously reported that the British study will state that plant fuels have played a "significant" part in pushing up food prices to record levels. . . .

[The World Bank] argues that the EU and US drive for biofuels has had by far the biggest impact on food supply and prices.

"Political leaders seem intent on suppressing and ignoring the strong evidence that biofuels are a major factor in recent food price rises," said Robert Bailey, policy adviser at Oxfam. "It is imperative that we have the full picture. While politicians concentrate on keeping industry lobbies happy, people in poor countries cannot afford enough to eat."

Rising food prices have pushed 100 [million] people worldwide below the poverty line, estimates the World Bank, and have sparked riots from Bangladesh to Egypt. Government ministers here have described higher food and fuel prices as "the first real economic crisis of globalisation".

President Bush has linked higher food prices to higher demand from India and China, but the leaked World Bank study disputes that: "Rapid income growth in developing countries has not led to large increases in global grain consumption and was not a major factor responsible for the large price increases."

Even successive droughts in Australia, calculates the report, have had a marginal impact. Instead, it argues that the EU [European Union] and US drive for biofuels has had by far the biggest impact on food supply and prices.

Since April [2008], all petrol and diesel in Britain has had to include 2.5% from biofuels. The EU has been considering raising that target to 10% by 2020, but is faced with mounting evidence that that will only push food prices higher.

"Without the increase in biofuels, global wheat and maize stocks would not have declined appreciably and price increases due to other factors would have been moderate," says the report. The basket of food prices examined in the study rose by 140% between 2002 and February [2008].

Production of biofuels has distorted food markets.

The report estimates that higher energy and fertiliser prices accounted for an increase of only 15%, while biofuels have been responsible for a 75% jump over that period.

Distortions in the Market

It argues that production of biofuels has distorted food markets in three main ways. First, it has diverted grain away from food for fuel, with over a third of US corn now used to produce ethanol and about half of vegetable oils in the EU going towards the production of biodiesel. Second, farmers have been encouraged to set land aside for biofuel production. Third, it has sparked financial speculation in grains, driving prices up higher.

Other reviews of the food crisis looked at it over a much longer period, or have not linked these three factors, and so arrived at smaller estimates of the impact from biofuels. But the report author, Don Mitchell, is a senior economist at the Bank and has done a detailed, month-by-month analysis of the surge in food prices, which allows much closer examination of the link between biofuels and food supply.

The report points out biofuels derived from sugarcane, which Brazil specializes in, have not had such a dramatic impact.

Supporters of biofuels argue that they are a greener alternative to relying on oil and other fossil fuels, but even that claim has been disputed by some experts, who argue that it does not apply to US production of ethanol from plants.

"It is clear that some biofuels have huge impacts on food prices," said Dr David King, the government's former chief scientific adviser. . . . "All we are doing by supporting these is subsiding higher food prices, while doing nothing to tackle climate change."

As Oil and Gas Prices Rise, Biofuels Can Solve the Food Crisis

Gordon Quaiattini

Gordon Quaiattini is president of the Canadian Renewable Fuels Association.

The world is experiencing a bio revolution. You can see it changing everything from medicine, clothing, auto parts, agricultural crops and fuels that power your car. Biotech medicines can now target specific cancer cells, bioengineering is dramatically increasing crop yields, and biofuels are starting to challenge the OPEC [Organization of Petroleum Exporting Countries] oil monopoly. Biotechnology is fuelling dramatic change around the world, but this change is not welcomed by everybody. The *National Post* recently published an alarming front-page article in which biofuels such as ethanol were blamed for damaging the global economy, causing starvation in the Third World, imperilling the food supply, destroying the environment and raping the world's forest.

Canadians deserve hearing the facts, beginning with the real cause of rising food prices. The benevolent, good-hearted people at OPEC who surely do not have any interests of their own at heart would love for you to believe that food prices are rising entirely because some corn is being used to make ethanol. The truth is that increases in food prices are rooted largely in increases in fuel prices. The cost of oil keeps rising— it's up an astonishing 100% in [2008] alone, increasing the cost of getting food from field to store to table. Increased demand in emerging economies such as China and India are impacting pricing for all commodities and yet somehow biofuels are singled out. Biofuels aren't part of the problem, they're part of the solution. Because of this new market and 21st-century agriculture practices—less fertilizer, less water, drought-resistant grains and increased yields on existing agriculture land—more crops are being planted and harvested, increasing supply at a time when, in the United States at least, a legislative cap actually restricts the amount of corn that can be directed toward ethanol production.

Ethanol and biodiesel are the most environmentally friendly and economically viable alternative to today's oil prices. Take a look around. Oil prices are entrenched at more than US$100 a barrel, leading to some of the highest gas prices this country and its motorists have ever seen.

Fossil Fuels and Global Warming

The global climate is being altered by emissions from fossil fuels. It seems clear that, as a planet, we need to grow beyond oil to pursue an alternative course that is better for our environment, for our economy and for our own wallets. That is the course offered by ethanol, biodiesel and other emerging biofuels.

The more biofuels we produce and use, the less reliant we will be on oil and OPEC and the more we will expose cartel members to the new (to them) idea of competition. It is now possible to imagine a world where fuels will compete against each other in a free market.

Biofuels will reduce the cost of harvesting and transporting food, . . . help to meet the world's growing energy demands . . . , and aid farmers.

The more biofuels we produce and use, the more we will help farmers in both the developed and the developing world. Sugar cane in Latin America and the Caribbean, and switchgrass and jatropha in Africa, are untapped biofuel resources that could help the Third World grow out of poverty. We are talking about a progressive agriculture policy that will help governments reduce or eliminate subsidies by making agriculture a more economical and free-market undertaking.

The more biofuels we produce and use, the less we will pollute our environment and contribute to global warming. The simple and well-documented truth is that ethanol and biodiesel burn cleaner than petroleum-based products. And according to data from Natural Resources Canada, the federal renewable fuels standard, which mandates a minimum percentage of biofuels in the fuel supply, will result in reductions to greenhouse gas emissions equivalent to removing more than one million cars from Canadian roads each and every year. What's more relevant going forward is that increased demand for ethanol will be met by new technologies such as cellulosic ethanol, which is made not from corn but from agriculture biomass, switchgrass, straw, and even wood and yard waste.

The True Promise of Biofuels

It is trendy these days for those with a political agenda or a divergent economic interest to label ethanol and its ilk as the source behind pretty much every problem on the global stage. Indeed, the *Post* headline would have you believe that biofuels have gone from "saviour to villain." But a more objective analysis would recognize the true promise of biofuels.

Policy leaders in Canada, the United States, Brazil and Europe rightly recognize biofuels will reduce the cost of harvesting and transporting food, economically bolster rural communities, help to meet the world's growing energy demands in a sustainable and environmentally responsible way, and aid farmers in their efforts to access new markets and achieve a new prosperity.

All that may not create a snappy headline. But eventually it will create a better world.

The Demand for Biofuels Is Not Directly Related to High Food Prices

Delta Farm Press Staff

Delta Farm Press *provides growers and agribusiness with in-depth coverage of the region's major crops plus the legislative, environmental, and regulatory issues that affect their businesses.*

There is no evidence that the nation's growing demand for biofuels and the crops needed to produce them are the culprits behind higher food prices at home or abroad, according to USDA's [US Department of Agriculture] top official.

Speaking at a food and fuel media briefing, Agriculture Secretary Ed Schafer acknowledged that higher demand for corn for ethanol and soybeans for biodiesel "has led to higher prices for those crops over the past couple of years. But we do not have a one-to-one relationship between higher prices for those commodities and what consumers are paying for foods at the retail level. There are many factors at work."

Schafer noted that USDA economists estimate "that only 3 percent of the more than 40 percent increase in world food prices this year [2008] is due to the increased demand on corn for ethanol."

Meanwhile in the United States, the year-to-year increase in food prices for U.S. consumers was much smaller than in the rest of the world, at 4 percent, and 1.5 percent higher than the average annual increase of 2.5 percent. Schafer does expect consumer prices to increase 5 percent [in 2008].

Meanwhile oil and food commodity prices are up almost 70 percent and almost 50 percent, respectively.

USDA chief economist Joe Glauber says only 20 percent of what consumers pay for food items can be attributed to the farm value of the underlying commodities. He believes much of the cost of food items comes from "labor costs, advertising, energy costs and other factors."

The External Factors Affecting Food Prices

Glauber said other factors affecting food prices include energy, weather, export restrictions and a rise in the standard of living in many developing countries.

"Global economic growth has been quite substantial over the last few years," he said. "The increasing gross domestic product in India and China has expanded demand, particularly for meat products, which has contributed to both a growth in livestock exports and demand for protein meals and soybean meal. And that this is projected to continue."

Droughts and other weather problems affected crops in Oceania, Australia, Ukraine, Canada and the European Union in 2007–2008.

And [in 2007], major rice- and wheat-producing countries imposed export restrictions, banned exports or increased export taxes, which limited supplies in the world marketplace, buoying prices.

Another major factor on food prices is energy costs, and their impact on food marketing and transportation costs.

Glauber also noted the impact of high costs on farmers. "On the input side, crop and livestock producers have been seeing much, much higher prices this year [2008]. One, fertilizer prices have really taken off, almost 67 percent. Fuel is up 43 percent, and feed costs up 23 percent over the first four months of 2007."

Glauber says USDA studies indicate that eliminating the blender credit for ethanol, as some politicians have asked for as a measure to reduce food prices, would result in a decline in corn prices of 10 percent to 15 percent.

But Schafer noted, "We don't want to do something here that's politically expedient, that sounds good, that makes headlines or 30-second sound bytes. We want to make sure that what we do here doesn't suppress production, but increases production so that we can feed people across the world.

"The policy choices we've made on biofuels will deliver long-term benefits. But we also have to recognize that there may be some short-term costs or dislocations involved, and we have to consider those costs in the light of the ultimate benefits that we hope to secure for the American people."

Cutting Crude Oil Use

Schafer noted that according to the International Energy Agency, biofuels production available to the United States and European markets over the last three years "has cut the consumption of crude oil by 1 million barrels a day. At today's prices, that's a savings of more than $120 million per day.

"Ethanol also brings environmental benefits. It gives us cleaner air by cutting tailpipe emissions of carbon monoxide and hydrocarbons that can cause ozone and smog. It also displaces benzene and other toxic ingredients of gasoline that would otherwise be burned at a greater rate. And by replacing MTBE as the blending agent of choice in gasoline, it has relieved us of water quality problems associated with MTBE while still boosting oxygen and octane contents of gasoline."

To address rising energy costs, Schafer stressed that the United States "needs to take steps to increase our domestic supply of traditional energy sources. We have vast untapped oil and gas reserves within our borders or just offshore. We could draw on those to help expand supply and bring down the cost of oil and therefore the price of food."

USDA is projecting a 33 percent increase in corn use in ethanol [in 2008], from 3 billion bushels to 4 billion bushels. Schafer noted that capacity and corn use for ethanol "should start to taper off as the corn-based ethanol production starts approaching the renewable fuels standard called for in the 2007 Energy Act."

Western Protectionist
Policies and Subsidies
Enable the Food Crisis

Conor Foley

Conor Foley is a humanitarian aid worker who has worked for a variety of human rights and humanitarian aid organizations.

Brazil's President [Luiz Inácio Lula da Silva] strongly defended his government's biofuels programme at the UN [United Nations] Food and Agricultural Organisation conference in Rome [in June 2008]. Since his remarks run directly counter to the *Guardian's* call to "use this summit to press the case for stopping biofuel production" in certain circumstances and it is worth elaborating why liberals in the north are taxing the patience of progressives in the south on this issue.

Brazilian ethanol, unlike its incredibly inefficient North American competitor, has had no demonstrable impact on the recent increase in food prices, as the relative stability of world sugar prices shows. Nor is the industry a direct threat to the Amazon rainforest. As Lula pointed out, "Our sugar plantations are 2,000km away from our rainforest. That is the distance from the Vatican to the Kremlin." Currently only about 1% of Brazil's arable land is given over to the production of biofuels and, while there are legitimate concerns that a rapid expansion of the industry could displace other crops, the Brazilian government is actually trying to regulate both the industry and working conditions within it.

Protectionist Policies Enable
the Food Crisis

"Ethanol is like cholesterol," Lula told the conference. "Good ethanol helps to tackle the pollution of the planet and is competitive. Bad ethanol depends on the fat of subsidies." He directly attacked the production of biofuels from maize and other forms of crop substitution by western farmers. He also said that he was "astonished, indignant and devastated" by the lobbying efforts of agro-business and the petroleum industry to keep their tariffs and subsidies, which are costing countries like Brazil dear in lost exports. "The fingers pointing at us with indignation are soiled with oil and charcoal." He argued that the only way of tackling the food crisis is to increase food supply and that some of the biggest obstacles to this are the protectionist policies of the rich world. The world would not be facing a food crisis, according to Lula, "if developing countries had been stimulated in a free-market context."

There is no doubt that one of the reasons for the sudden rise in food prices has been the decision by many farmers in Europe and North America to switch production to growing cereals which can be converted to biofuels. As Chris Goodall has pointed out, about 100[million] tonnes of maize from [2008's] US crop will be diverted into ethanol refineries, which means one in 20 of all cereal grains produced in the world will end up in the petrol tank of US cars. This is an increase of a third on 2007's figure and has obviously had a knock-on effect on the supply chain. Rising oil prices have also increased the production and shipping costs of food—as well as providing farmers with a greater incentive to produce for this market.

The average European cow receives more financial support than half the world's population has to live on.

The second reason, it is generally accepted, why prices have risen, is that people in Asia and Latin America are eating more meat, which is a consequence of rising living standards. However, the Malthusian view that links rising food prices directly to population growth is not supported by the facts, since the price spike has occurred while rate of increase of the world's population is currently slowing. Those who argue that there are simply too many people on the planet, also need to explain what they propose to do about it. Fortunately, there is a clear link between rising incomes and decreasing birth rates, which should eventually stabilise population growth. The far bigger problem is not that there may come a time in the future when there is not enough food to feed everyone, but the fact that every single year at the moment around 3.5 million children lose their lives as a direct result of malnutrition.

The Problem of Income, Not Food Scarcity

The point Lula has made repeatedly when defending Brazil's biofuels programme is that: "The problem with world hunger is not a shortage of food but a shortage of income." He called for a "radical change in ways of thinking and acting" about food production to "increase food supply, open up markets and wipe out subsidies". He also said that the "cutting-edge technology" which Brazil has developed to "bring together the earth, sun and labour" in a "golden revolution" could be exported to Africa to help tackle poverty as well as global warming and food and energy shortages.

As Kevin Watkins [director of the UN's Human Development Report Office] has argued, The US government is currently spending $7 [billion] a year in subsidizing maize-based biofuels, which has been a huge boost to American agrobusiness but has had zero benefits for reduced carbon emissions. France alone received a subsidy of $12bn for the European Union's notorious Common Agricultural Policy [in 2007], and the average European cow receives more financial support than half the world's population has to live on. This money could instead be used far more efficiently to increase food production by strengthening the development of agriculture in the south. Instead it is often used for precisely the opposite purpose. One of the reasons why so many of the world's poorest countries remain both poor and particularly vulnerable to sudden food price rises is that the dumping of food by Europe and North America has wiped out many local markets.

This is the key issue in the debate, which some liberals and environmentalists in the rich world seem either not to have fully grasped or simply want to ignore. The World Trade Organisation [WTO] is not the main enemy. Indeed it is difficult to see how the issue can be tackled without an agreement, which in reality can only be achieved through the WTO, that stops rich countries dumping surpluses, opens up their agricultural markets and supports the development of agriculture in poor countries. You do not show solidarity with poor people by supporting policies which keep them in poverty and it is obscene to pretend otherwise.

Can Biotechnology Solve the Global Food Crisis?

Chapter Preface

Humans have sought new methods to improve crop and livestock yields from ancient times, using crossbreeding to produce stronger varieties and introducing new fertilizers or pest control techniques to ensure the health of their land and harvests. In the twentieth century, as the sizes of farms grew to unprecedented scales, new and controversial technologies emerged that promised to increase food volumes and save crops from unwanted pests safely and efficiently. In the face of the global food crisis, with communities suffering dire shortages of staple grains, many economists and agronomists—those who study crop production and soil management—have argued that the only solution to the problem is to embrace these tools of modern biotechnology as the best and most efficient way to ensure that there is enough food to feed the world.

Biotechnology in a general sense refers to the use of living organisms to modify human health and the environment. In agriculture, modern biotechnologists make precise genetic changes to plants and animals used for food to impart what are believed to be beneficial traits. These traits then cause them to produce higher yields, be less prone to disease, or to be more nutritious and thus benefit human consumers. Some of the methods of modern biotechnology include introducing or deleting a particular gene or genes to produce plants, animals, and microorganisms with novel traits. This genetic engineering produces genetically modified organisms, or GMOs.

Promoters of biotechnology know that mere mention of "GMOs" is enough to make many environmental and food activists balk, and to argue that "Frankenfoods," as they are called, are a scourge that cannot possibly benefit humanity. However, Nobel Prize-winning agronomist Norman Borlaug insists this is not the case, asserting that not only are such foods safe and healthful but necessary to combat starvation that persists around the world. He believes that Western protestors who hold a romanticized view of sustainable farming practices have done a disservice to the global poor, whose best hope of sustainable yields is from crops grown with the aid of molecular biotechnology. Economist Jeffrey Sachs echoes this view, saying that many poor farmers in the Third World are hampered because of their crude farming methods that produce little yield, and that using biotechnology is a quick and efficient way to ensure that they do more than eke out a bare subsistence from their land.

Other experts, however, including the Union of Concerned Scientists, do not regard biotechnology as offering the benefits that Borlaug and Sachs claim. They argue that the notion that biotechnology increases crop yields is simply not borne out by the facts, and in fact they do more harm than good. Others as well see that there is good reason to reject the promotion of genetically modified food, because its impact on human health has not been adequately studied. Indian environmental activist Vandana Shiva has noted that biotechnology has been heavily promoted to rural farmers in India in a way that has been immoral and devastating to the community. Forced to buy genetically modified grains that do not re-seed themselves, farmers become beholden to large multinational corporations whose interest is not in ensuring that communities feed themselves but in exploiting the land as an economic commodity. While these corporations continue to take in record earnings, the global crisis they purport to help has only gotten worse. And the crisis will continue to deepen, she says, unless communities take back their traditional farming practices, which for centuries have sustained them, and reclaim the notions that the earth and food are for people and not for profit.

Biotechnology Is Essential to Feed the World's Growing Population

Norman E. Borlaug

Norman E. Borlaug is an agronomist. He was awarded the Nobel Peace Prize in 1970 in recognition of his contributions to world peace through increasing food supply.

All of life involves weighing risks against benefits. Through our own experience, and by observing that of others, we assess the risks of familiar activities and, sometimes almost subconsciously, we adapt to them. A child soon learns—sometimes painfully—about the high risk of touching a hot stove. Usually without a great deal of thought, we run the hazard of shark attacks at the beach. Academics and insurance company experts have been able to quantify the risks of, say, smoking a pack of cigarettes a day, commuting to work by car, or undergoing cardiac surgery.

Assessing the Risks and Benefits of Technology

Risk is more problematic when we are confronted with unfamiliar activities or products. In the absence of sufficient experience (what scientists would call "data") to make a confident assessment of risk, we tend to become anxious and to compensate for our lack of knowledge by overestimating the risk.

The authors [Henry I. Miller and Gregory Conko of *The Frankenfood Myth*] use an apposite contemporary example to illustrate public policy run amok—the regulation in the United States and abroad of the new biotechnology, or gene-splicing, which has great potential to improve plants and microorganisms for agriculture and food production. Henry I. Miller and Gregory Conko make a persuasive case not only that the benefits of the technology far exceed its risk but also that there has been an abject failure in the formulation of public policy. The result has been, they argue correctly, gross overregulation of the technology and its products, disincentives to research and development, and fewer choices and inflated prices for consumers.

As a plant pathologist and breeder, I have seen how the skeptics and critics of the new biotechnology wish to postpone the release of improved crop varieties in the hope that another year's, or another decade's, worth of testing will offer more data, more familiarity, more comfort. But more than a half-century in the agricultural sciences has convinced me that we should use the best that is at hand, while recognizing its imperfections and limitations. Far more often than not, this philosophy has worked, in spite of constant pessimism and scaremongering by critics.

I am reminded of our using the technology at hand to defeat the specter of famine in India and Pakistan in the 1950s and early 1960s. Most "experts" thought that mass starvation was inevitable, and environmentalists like Stanford's Paul Ehrlich predicted that hundreds of millions would die in Africa and Asia within just a few years "in spite of any crash programs embarked upon." The funders of our work were cautioned against wasting resources on a problem that was insoluble.

Nevertheless, in 1963, the Rockefeller Foundation and the Mexican government formed the International Maize and Wheat Improvement Center (known by its Spanish acronym CIMMYT) and sent my team to South Asia to teach local farmers how to cultivate high-yield wheat varieties. As a result, Pakistan became self-sufficient in wheat production by 1968 and India a few years later.

As we created what became known as the "Green Revolution," we confronted bureaucratic chaos, resistance from local seed breeders, and centuries of farmers' customs, habits, and superstitions. We surmounted these difficult obstacles because something new *had* to be done. Who knows how many would have starved if we had delayed commercializing the new high-yielding cereal varieties and improved crop management practices until we could perform tests to rule out every hypothetical problem, and test for vulnerability, to every conceivable type of disease and pest? How much land, for nature and wildlife habitat, and how much topsoil would have been lost if the more traditional, low-yield practices had not been supplanted?

At the time, Forrest Frank Hill, a Ford Foundation vice president, told me, "Enjoy this now, because nothing like it will ever happen to you again. Eventually the naysayers and the bureaucrats will choke you to death, and you won't be able to get permission for more of these efforts." Hill was right. His prediction anticipated the gene-splicing era that would arrive decades later.... The naysayers and bureaucrats have now come into their own. If our new varieties had been subjected to the kinds of regulatory strictures and requirements that are being inflicted upon the new biotechnology, they would *never* have become available.

The Record of High-Yield Agriculture

From 1950 to 1992, the world's grain output rose from 692 million tons produced on 1.70 billion acres of cropland to 1.9 billion tons on 1.73 billion acres of cropland—an increase in yield of more than 150 percent. Without high-yield agriculture, either millions would have starved or increases in food output would have been realized only through drastic expansion of acres under cultivation—with losses of pristine wilderness a hundred times greater than all the losses to urban and suburban expansion.

Today, we confront a similar problem: feeding the anticipated global population of more than eight billion people in the coming quarter of a century. The world has or will soon have the agricultural technology available to meet this challenge. The new biotechnology can help us to do things that we could not do before, and to do it in a more precise, predictable, and efficient way. The crucial question today is whether farmers and ranchers will be permitted to use that technology. Extremists in the environmental movement are doing everything they can to stop scientific progress in its tracks, and their allies in the regulatory agencies are more than eager to help.

No negative health or environmental effects have been observed [from gene-spliced, insect-resistant corn].

We owe a debt of gratitude to the environmental movement for raising global awareness of the importance of air and water quality and of wildlife and wilderness preservation. It is ironic, therefore, that if the platform of anti-biotechnology extremists were to be adopted, it would have grievous consequences for both the environment and humanity. If the naysayers do manage to stop agricultural biotechnology, they might actually precipitate the famines and the crisis of global biodiversity they have been predicting for nearly forty years.

The Anti-Biotech Movement

For a decade, the United States has produced ever-larger quantities of gene-spliced, insect-resistant corn that yields as much as or more than the best traditional hybrids but with far less need for chemical pesticides. No negative health or environmental effects have been observed. Yet there is an immensely strong, rabid anti-biotech lobby, especially in Europe, where activists have convinced many governments to thwart new approvals and have opposed the use of gene-spliced corn and soybeans as food aid in famine-stricken parts of Africa and Asia. Recently, in the southern African countries of Zambia, Zimbabwe, and Angola, where many people arc dying of starvation, this anti-biotech movement has helped to persuade government authorities to refuse food aid from the United States because it contains gene-spliced corn. But the risk-benefit characteristics of gene-splicing in general, and of this insect-resistant corn in particular, are extraordinarily favorable; this rejection is an obscene exaggeration of risk.

Tragically, this is not an isolated case. There are many other examples of overreaction and resistance to technology. The American Council on Science and Health has documented a series of twenty cases—including pesticides on cranberries in 1959, the supposed hazards of cyclamates in 1969, "agent orange" in 1979, and Alar® on Pacific coast apples in 1989—in which scare stories trumpeted by the media became widely known and accepted but later were shown to be of little or no consequence. The resistance to gene splicing is yet another sordid episode in this larger anti-technology, junk-science movement.

The world cannot feed all its 6.3 billion people from organic farms.

In spite of the many powerful and precise new tools and the greater health and well-being that science and technology have offered us, our society has become overly risk averse. We obsess over impurities that are detectable at levels of one part per billion, for example, while not so many years ago we would have declared a product pure if adulterants were present at less than one part per five hundred thousand. Not infrequently, regulators worry about levels of contamination not because they are worrisome but because they are detectable. They regulate not because they should but because they can.

This is both foolish and destructive. Sometimes greater analytical sensitivity requires greater intellectual perspicacity.

We Resist Change at our Peril

Regulators are not alone in their demands for ever-increasing margins of safety. It seems we are born with an instinct to resist change and to regard what is new with suspicion, while forgetting the faults and risks that were readily tolerated in the past and that were eliminated or ameliorated by new technologies; chlorination of water, pasteurization, and vaccination readily come to mind. Our very wealth and well-being, made possible by technology, now seem to offer the luxury of forgoing additional advances. But we are hard put to equal the immortal observation of the head of the U.S. patent office at the dawning of the twentieth century who suggested that the office be closed because surely everything possible had already been invented.

We must be more rational about our approach to risks. We need to think in broader terms, recognizing, for example, that the world cannot feed all its 6.3 billion people from organic farms or power all its cities and industries by wind and solar energy.

Although we must be prudent in assessing new technologies, these assessments must not be based on overly conservative—or overtly inaccurate—assumptions or be swayed by the anti-business, anti-establishment, anti-globalization agendas of a few activists, or by the self-interest of bureaucrats. They must be based on good science and good sense. It is easy to forget that science offers more than a body of knowledge and a process for adding new knowledge. It tells us not only what we know but what we don't know. It identifies areas of uncertainty and offers an estimate of how great and how critical that uncertainty may be. . . .

The [leading] problems of the new biotechnology . . . have arisen not from limits of the technology itself or from the science underlying it but from the machinations and peregrinations of policy makers. We must begin to solve *those* problems before it is too late.

Modern Technologies Can Foster Success in Poor Farming Communities

Jeffrey Sachs

Jeffrey Sachs is professor of economics and director of the Earth Institute at Columbia University.

Many poor, food-importing countries around the world have become desperate [since the beginning of 2008] because global prices of rice, wheat and maize have doubled. Hundreds of millions of poor people, who already spend a large share of their daily budget on food, are being pushed to the edge. Food riots are mounting.

But many poor countries can grow more food themselves, because their farmers are producing far below what is technologically possible. In some cases, with appropriate government action, they could double or even triple food production in just a few years.

The idea is basic and well known. Traditional farming uses few inputs and gets poor yields. Poor peasants use their own seeds from the preceding season, lack fertilizer, depend on rain rather than irrigation, and have little if any mechanization beyond a traditional hoe. Their farms are small, perhaps one hectare or less.

Increasing Yields

Under traditional agricultural conditions, the yields of grain—rice, wheat, maize, sorghum or millet—are usually around one tonne per hectare for one planting season per year. For a farm family of five or six living on one hectare, this means extreme poverty, and for their country it means reliance on expensive food imports, including food aid.

The solution is to increase grain yields to at least two tonnes—and in some places to three or more tonnes—per hectare. If water can be managed through irrigation, this could be combined with multicropping (multiple harvests per year) to produce a crop during the dry season. Higher and more frequent yields mean less poverty in farm families and lower food prices for cities.

If farmers can be helped to obtain simple technologies, income can rise, and they can accumulate bank balances and collateral.

The key to increasing yields is to ensure that even the poorest farmers have access to improved seed varieties (usually "hybrid" seeds created by scientific selection of seed varieties), chemical fertilizers, organic matter to replenish soil nutrients and, where possible, small-scale irrigation methods, such as a pump to lift water from a nearby well. There is nothing magic about this combination of high-yield seeds, fertilizer and small-scale irrigation. It is the key to the worldwide increase in food production since the 1960s.

The problem is that these improved inputs have bypassed the poorest farmers and the poorest countries. When peasants lack their own saving accounts and collateral, they are unable to borrow from banks to buy seeds, fertilizer and irrigation equipment. As a result, they grow food the traditional way, often earning little or nothing from their harvest, because it's not even enough to keep their families alive.

Short-Term Assistance

History has shown that government action is required to help the poorest farmers escape the low-yield poverty trap. If farmers can be helped to obtain simple technologies, income can rise, and they can accumulate bank balances and collateral. With a bit of temporary help, perhaps lasting around five years, farmers can build up enough wealth to obtain inputs on a market basis, either through direct purchases from savings or through bank loans.

Government-run agricultural banks in poor countries once not only financed inputs, but also provided agricultural advice and spread new seed technologies.

Of course, there were abuses, such as the allocation of public credits to richer farmers rather than to needy ones, or the prolonged subsidization of inputs even after farmers became credit-worthy. And, in many cases, government agricultural banks went bankrupt.

Still, the financing of inputs played a huge and positive role in helping the poorest farmers to escape poverty and dependency on food aid.

During the debt crisis of the 1980s and 1990s, the IMF [International Monetary Fund] and the World Bank forced dozens of poor food-importing countries to dismantle these state systems. Poor farmers were told to fend for themselves, to let "market forces" provide for inputs. This was a profound mistake: There were no such market forces.

Poor farmers lost access to fertilizers and improved seed varieties. They could not obtain bank financing. To its credit, the World Bank recognized this mistake in a scathing internal evaluation of its long-standing agricultural policies [in 2007].

The Need for Public Financing

The time has come to re-establish public financing systems that enable small farmers in the poorest countries, notably those farming on two hectares or less, to gain access to needed inputs of high-yield seeds, fertilizer and small-scale irrigation. Malawi has done this for the past three seasons and has doubled its food production as a result. Other low-income countries should follow suit.

Importantly, the World Bank, under its new president, Robert Zoellick, has stepped forward to help finance this new approach. If the bank provides grants to poor countries to help small peasant farmers gain access to improved inputs, then it will be possible for those countries to increase their food production in a short period of time.

Donor governments, including the oil-rich countries of the Middle East, should help finance the World Bank's new efforts. The world should set as a practical goal of doubling grain yields in low-income Africa and similar regions (such as Haiti) during the next five years [2008–2013]. That's achievable if the World Bank, donor governments and poor countries direct their attention to the urgent needs of the world's poorest farmers.

Biotechnology and Agribusiness Create Cultural and Economic Devastation

Vandana Shiva, Maria Armoudian, and Ankine Aghassian

Vandana Shiva is a physicist and environmental activist. Maria Armoudian is a singer/songwriter and a commissioner on the environment for the City of Los Angeles. Ankine Aghassian is a human rights activist. Together Armoudian and Aghassian produce the Insighters *show for KPFK Radio in Los Angeles.*

Policy-makers are finally grappling with the growing global food and water crises that are upon us. While they grope for answers, Vandana Shiva reminds them that it was their wild economic schemes that created these crises in the first place.

The globalized economic structure is simply incompatible with the basic physics of the planet and the principles of democratic governance, she says. And until we align the economic system with those of the ecological system, the problems will only get worse. . . .

The Global Marketplace and the Globe

AlterNet: Much of your writing and speaking has focused on our economic structure's incompatibility with the ecological functioning of the earth. Talk about that incompatibility.

Vandana Shiva: One aspect of the inconsistency is between the principles of Gaia, the principles of soil, the ecology, renewability, how the atmosphere cleans itself and the laws of the global marketplace. The global marketplace is driven by the World Bank and the World Trade Organization (WTO) and the illogic of so-called "free trade," which is totally not free. [The result of this incompatibility] is the current food crisis: The more agriculture is "liberalized," the greater the food scarcity, the higher the food prices and the more people will go hungry.

Never has there been this rate of escalation in food prices worldwide as we witness now with the global integration of the food economies under the coercive and bullying force of the WTO.

You have said, in the past, that these activities are done in the name of improving human welfare. But instead, poverty and dispossession have increased. Where do we see this the most?

We see the worst dispossession in the countries of the South—tragically—those countries that could feed themselves. India, for example, was food self-sufficient. We were able to feed our people with a universal distribution system, afford-able food for all, and agriculture policies that put food first. Small farmers could make a living.

But a decade and a half of globalization's perverse rules have led to 200,000 farmers committing suicide because they can't make a living anymore—all their money goes to make profit for Monsanto or Cargill. Meanwhile, with the economy's so-called growth, people are starving. Per capita entitlement to food has dropped in a decade and half from 177 kg to 152 kg per year.

This contradicts the false propaganda being spread about the reason prices are rising. They say it is because Indians are getting richer and Indians are eating more. Well, some Indians are getting richer, but they're not eating more. There's a limit to how much you can eat. And the handful of billionaires buys a few more private jet planes and builds a few more pri-vate mansions. [But in reality], the average Indian is eating less. The average child has a bigger chance today of dying of hunger. The Cargill's of the world have a stranglehold of the world's economy; they're harvesting super-profits while people die of hunger.

Globalization and Increased Malnutrition

You talk about India being worse off, but many economists— including those on the political left—say that places like China and India are, overall, actually improving. But you say that is not true.

It's not true. India, under the perverse growth of globalization, has beaten out Africa in the number of hungry people. While we have 9.2 percent growth measured by GNP [gross national product] and GDP [gross domestic product], 50 percent of our children have very severe malnutrition. Fifty percent of deaths for children under five are due to lack of food. That's about a million kids per year.

Food ultimately is not produced in the speculation and commodity exchanges . . . It is produced by hard working women and men.

That is a considerable change that I don't think the world is seeing.

That's because the media orchestrates every analysis and interpretation. They would like this crisis to look like a success of globalization, and they would like to offer more globalization as a solution. In fact, the World Bank has said there should be more liberalized trade. Before the WTO was formed, we had protests with 500,000 farmers on the streets of Bangalore in 1993 to say that this is a recipe for starvation, for destroying agriculture, self-reliance and food security. And the General Agreement on Trade and Tariffs—before the WTO was born—had a press conference to say that globalization will make food affordable for all.

They forget that food ultimately is not produced in the speculation and commodity exchanges controlled by Cargill in Chicago. It is produced by hard working women and men working with the soil and sun. And if you destroy the capacity of the people to work the land and the capacity of soil to produce, you're going to have hunger. The tragedy is that the hunger of today and the rise of food [prices] is the result of globalization policies, and it is being implemented on a global scale. Unless we bring local food sovereignty and "food democracy" back into the picture, we will not have a solution to this.

Destroying the Real Free Economy

You're talking about basic ecological principles here. But there are two other aspects about food shortages that are being discussed. One of them is that among some societies, such as China, the diet is changing, which contributes to food shortage. Reportedly, after being exposed to western diets, they are eating more meat which requires an enormous amount of grain—normally fed to people—to instead be fed to cattle. Do you see this as part of the problem?

Well, I can definitely say that is not true for India. Vegetarian India will stay vegetarian India—rich or poor, integrated globally or not integrated globally. And the Chinese have always eaten meat. The difference is that now they are integrated into the global production system: It is factory farming that feeds grain to chicken and pigs and cows.

No indigenous culture—or India—has fed grain to animals. Animals have fed on what humans could not eat. Global agribusiness, which makes huge money out of the feed industry, is creating this pressure while destroying what I would call the "real free economy"—the free-range cattle, the free range chicken—and replacing it with prison factories for animals. In fact, in my interpretation, even the Avian flu is being used to violently shut down small economies, the free economies of Asian peasants, and turning them into Tyson and Cargill factory farming systems.

What about the role of climate change in this global food crisis?

Climate change and agricultural food crises do have a connection. In fact, my next book is precisely about this connection. Industrial farming—driven by agribusiness in order to sell more chemicals, pesticides, and costly seeds to farmers—is heavily responsible for emissions of greenhouse gases such as methane from factory farms, nitrogen oxide from chemically fertilized soil and fossil fuels from mechanized farming systems.

Biodiverse systems actually produce more food.

Further, the long distance trade is responsible for adding food miles, which adds more carbon emissions. Taken together, more than 25 percent of climate instability is being caused by unsustainable farming that [simultaneously] displaces small peasants, creates poverty and bad food. So, tomorrow we could solve 25 percent of the planet's climate instability if we returned to ecological agriculture as the earth wants it, farming according to 10,000 years of wisdom that evolved from the third world.

Research that we are undertaking now shows a 200 percent higher level of carbon return and 10 times higher level of moisture retention. So if increased drought is one consequence of climate change, what you need is sorted organic matter, not more chemical fertilizers. We have two issues pertaining to climate change: We need to get rid of emissions from agriculture and long-distance transport.

This means ecological farming, localization of the food system and only importing what can't be grown locally—not forcing imports as the U.S has done on India. It has forced us to buy wheat, give up our mustard and coconut oil and to live on soya. These trade factors are "forcings" that are causing more damage to our climate and destroying our food culture, nutrition and access to food.

Finally, biodiverse systems actually produce more food. It is an illusion that because there's a food crisis, we must have [genetically modified food] spread around the world. First, genetically-engineered crops don't produce more food. And secondly, they make the soil more vulnerable to climate change. They are herbicide resistant and toxin traps. That is not a yield increase. . . .

Water Scarcity and Privatization

We should also talk about water scarcity. There are major water wars occurring and considerable concern about the future of water. Do you think that water scarcity is being created largely by the phenomenon of privatization or is it resulting from climate change and other such phenomena?

Water scarcity [is] being created by non-sustainable systems of production for both food and textile. Every industrial activity has huge water demands. Industrial agriculture requires ten times more water to produce the same amount of food than ecological farming does. And the "green revolution" was not so green because it created demand for large dams and mining of groundwater.

Industrial agriculture has depleted water resources. In addition, as water has become polluted and depleted, a handful of industry saw water as a way of making super-profits by privatizing it. They are privatizing it in two ways. The first is through buying up entire civic, municipal distribution. The big players in this are Bechtel, Suez and Vivendi.

And interestingly, wherever they go, they face protests. Bechtel was thrown out of Bolivia. Suez wanted to take Delhi's water supply, but we had a movement for water democracy and did not allow them to take over. But there's a second kind of privatization, which is more insidious—and that is the plastic water bottle. Coca-Cola and Pepsi are leading in this privatization. But in India where Coca-Cola was stealing water, I worked with a small group of village women, and they shut their plant down. Across India, these giant corporations are taking between 1.5 to 2 million liters of water a day and leaving behind a water famine.

Unfortunately, governance today is run by corporations not the people. Every step of deepening the market economy is a depletion of democracy.

Given what is happening as a result of climate change, would we still face a water crisis without these practices?

We would not be facing water problems if people have been allowed to have their economies, to practice sustainability and to live their lives. Every step in the water crisis is due to greed. As the water becomes increasingly scarce, the corporations who control the water become richer, it is the same with food. As food becomes scarce, the corporations controlling food become richer. That is the paradox of the global economy. Growth shows up in the profits of corporations while in the real world, the resources from which they make their profits, shrink.

Globalization Threatens Democracy

You have also suggested that these same economic principles are incompatible with the sustenance of democratic governance.

There are many levels at which a market economy called corporate globalization has to kill democracy in order to survive. Take the birth of World Trade Organization (WTO), an undemocratic institution. There are no negotiations on the rules it imposes. These rules are created undemocratically. Then, every time these rules are implemented, there are protests. Normally in democracy, if the will of people say change this policy, governments change. Unfortunately, governance today is run by corporations not the people. Every step of deepening the market economy is a depletion of democracy. Our very governments have been stolen from us, and we have to use democracy to counter these rules, this paradigm, and the absolute destruction [it causes].

Describe your alternative vision that could replace what we currently have.

I try to articulate an alternative vision in terms of a democracy. Global market economy makes the first citizen the corporation. The rest of us are slaves, second class citizens. Secondly, it creates an identity for the human species as consumers in a global supermarket. We are no longer creators and producers. We are just consumers of goods that corporations bring to us from the place where they can manufacture them—at the highest cost to the environment and workers.

What we need is a reclaiming of who we are as human beings. We are first and foremost citizens of this beautiful planet. Our first duty is to protect this planet. And out of that flows the rights to the earth, air, water and food that the earth gives us. Those gifts are common resources, not commodities, private property or intellectual property. They are the commons of the earth and all of us have equal access to it. Nobody can interfere in the access of a person to their share of water, land and air. That interference is a violation of the rules of Gaia and the rules of democracy.

But the polluting industry has privatized even the air by first putting their pollutants into it and then by the carbon trade. They're basically are saying that because we polluted the atmosphere, we own it. So we can pollute as much as we want and then buy up clean credits from someone else who is not polluting. The commons and the recovery of commons is vital to earth democracy. It's at the heart of sustainability of the earth and democratic functioning of society.

Private Property and Communal Resources

Do property rights fit into this vision of the commons?

Most private property rights have been carved out of the shared resources of the earth. In India we say "land belongs to creation." We can use it and have "use rights," but that is different from ownership and tradable rights. It is British colonialism that created private property in land the way it is now practiced.

Now, the World Bank is trying to create private property in land among indigenous communities. Water was never property either, but today, they are trying to change that. Seeds were meant to be shared and distributed, not treated as property. Intellectual property rights are as recent as the World Trade Organization and need to be eliminated because they are inconsistent with life [principles]. A world of the future governed by intellectual property rights over seed in Monsanto's hands is a future where biodiversity will be destroyed, farmers will be wiped out and there will be no food worth eating.

You've also been involved in the "slow food" movement and organic farming.

I was just elected Vice President of Slow Food [International], and I chair an international commission on the future of food, a commission started by the region of Tuscany in Italy. I convinced the [founder], Carlo Petrini, to recognize that food does not begin in the kitchen or in the chef's hands. It begins in the farmers' fields. One of the contributions that I and my colleagues have made in the seed-saving and organic farming movements is the recognition that biodiversity, organic farming and small-scale agriculture produces more food. It is a myth created by industrial agriculture and agribusiness that monocultures and chemical farming produce more food. They use more energy and chemicals, and do not produce more nutrition per acre. In fact, they use ten times more energy inputs than they produce as food. So with the food crisis, it is vital that we move to efficient food systems that also give us better quality food.

How would we carry your vision and language into actual political and farming structure?

In countries like India, it's not a case of vision being translated into practice. It's defending a practice that's being destroyed by a perverse vision. For us, it is defending the rights of small peasants. That's where lot of my energy goes. An India of the villages was Gandhi's dream and is my dream. But I do not see India surviving if her villages and her food capacity are wiped out. In the Northern countries like the United States farmers have already been uprooted. We need more farms producing more locally-grown foods. This country that can subsidize biofuel and chemicals should instead subsidize the return of small farmers to the land. This would solve much of the unemployment problem too.

Biotechnology Is Ineffective and Potentially Disastrous

Sam Urquhart

Sam Urquhart is a journalist from London. He has written on environmental and social justice issues and is an activist with the Campaign Against Climate Change.

In [June 2008], the battle over the world's food supply moved to Rome where the UN's [United Nations'] Food and Agriculture Organization (FAO) held an international summit to discuss rising food prices, climate change and biofuels cultivation. There was much coverage of the summit in the world's media, often focusing on the high profile appearance of Zimbabwean president Robert Mugabe or the Iranian president Mahmud Ahmedinejad, yet few commentators looked into the rotten heart of the exercise.

The Rome Summit turned out to be a sham, which resulted in a declaration that let biofuels producers off the hook, opened up space for the world-wide spread of GM [genetically modified] seeds and for the further liberalization of agricultural markets. Alternative policy choices being proposed by a broad array of food sovereignty campaigners, peasant farmers' groups, economists and human rights organizations were not simply crowded out, they were actively suppressed.

The crisis itself certainly merited attention. Global food prices have risen 83% [between 2005 and 2007] while recent price rises have only accelerated this trend. According to the FAO, there has been a 45% increase in their world food price index [between September 2007 and June 2008] while the *Economist*'s own food price index puts wheat prices 130% above [2007's] levels.

Sam Urquhart, "Making a Profit Out of The Food Crisis: From A Brave New World Bank to Monsanto," *Toward Freedom*, July 17, 2008. Copyright © 2005 Toward Freedom. Reproduced by permission of the author.

139

These developments have hit the developing world particularly hard, and not just because poorer people spend a relatively higher proportion of their income on food. Previous bouts of neoliberal structural adjustment at the request of financial institutions already placed many national economies in a precarious state and often led directly to higher food prices.

This general situation combined with recent price rises has contributed to the wave of food riots that has taken hold in countries as diverse as Haiti, Indonesia, Mexico, Bangladesh, Burkina Faso, Egypt, Senegal, Cameroon, Morocco, Yemen, Somalia and the Philippines—showing with crystal clarity the global scale of the problem.

A Brave New World Bank?

These food riots, and the specter of many millions of hungry, radicalized peasants and slum dwellers has spurred the World Bank and UN to react. However, with crisis has come opportunity. As Naomi Klein discusses in her book *The Shock Doctrine*—neoliberalism works best when societies are prepared for its implementation via societal "shock." Debt and hunger—both products of rising food and oil prices—are generating just such a shock. So while there is a fear of instability, there is also a sense of opportunity.

Critics of the World Bank have long questioned its motives in dispensing aid to poorer nations and have attacked the conditionalities that it has attached to its loans as a means of opening up under-developed economies to corporate predation, yet the IMF [International Monetary Fund] and World Bank have stumbled in recent years. This has partly been due to their failed policies, but also due to a credit glut brought on by spiraling oil prices. Smaller nations have not needed the services of the global institutions and their power has begun to wane. But with the credit crunch and rising food prices, some nations are headed back to the trough.

Eric Holt-Gimenez of Food First thinks that this represents an opportunity for the World Bank to regain some of its lost influence. As he told me, "For the World Bank, the food crisis comes at a perfect time." With the credit glut and countries turning away from the Bank, "the challenge became how to get countries of the global south to borrow again."

Rising food prices have fortunate effects for the Bank. As Holt-Gimenez continued, "The world food crisis solves both the problem of over-accumulation of finance capital and the problem of overproduction of grain, that neither biofuels nor the beef industry is capable of sopping up."

[The United Nations] shut its ears to alternative notions of agricultural development, turning its summit into a rubber-stamping exercise that put profits firmly before people and land.

Hence, when the battle for the world's fields and bellies shifted to Rome, the World Bank launched a PR [public relations] blitz, announcing the launch of a $1.2 billion "fast-track facility for [the] food crisis" including $200 million in grants "targeted at the vulnerable in the world's poorest countries." Haiti ($10 million), Liberia ($10 million) and Djibouti ($5 million) have since become the first nations to receive such assistance, although as Bank chief Robert Zoellick says, this will be part of "longer-term solution that must involve many countries and institutions," including the FAO, meeting in Rome.

But this was simply PR. Moves to restructure the global economy to protect small producers from market fluctuations and the predations of agribusiness giants were strikingly absent from the Bank's response, just as they were absent from the outcome of the Rome summit itself.

Sidelining the World

This absence was not because of a lack of well-articulated alternatives. A bottom-up alternative to corporate-led agricultural globalization is, in fact, readily available. As a recent statement from the campaigning NGO [non-governmental organization] GRAIN puts it, "Peasant organisations and their allies have clear, viable ideas about how to organize production and services and how to run markets and even regional and international trade. Ditto for labor unions and the urban poor, who have an important role to play in defining food policy." These groups were all present in Rome, holding the parallel *Terra Preta* summit to air their ideas and causes.

Unfortunately, the problem was that over at the main summit those in power simply weren't listening. The FAO shut its ears to alternative notions of agricultural development, turning its summit into a rubber-stamping exercise that put profits firmly before people and land.

This is shown in heartbreaking detail by the FAO's own preparatory documents for the summit. As with all gatherings of international institutions, the FAO consulted its "stakeholders"—although some decidedly more closely than others. When it consulted its "civil society" stakeholders, the result was perhaps the most thorough analysis of how to solve the food crisis yet delivered.

From raising awareness of consumption patterns in the developed world, promoting sustainable farming practices, setting up a framework to tackle climate change without harming rural livelihoods to disseminating information on climate change and methods of cultivation, the civil society stakeholders made some sensible recommendations for the FAO.

It recommended that bio-energy (in the form of sustainably harvested local sources such as plant products or animal dung) be promoted instead of biofuels. It argued that the FAO should demand that governments adopt measures to prevent the dispossession of rural people for plantations and carbon offset schemes. It proposed that the FAO promote seed sharing and document and disseminate indigenous knowledge. It advocated the protection of biodiversity by local peoples, while it also called for the Right to Food to guide global agricultural policies, not the right to profit.

It was roundly ignored.

The Summit Was Without Substance

Patrick Mulvany, senior policy adviser at UK based NGO Practical Action (and a participant in the civil society consultation) told me that at a June 2nd [2008] plenary meeting with FAO officials, activists from Via Campesina attacked the FAO process. Speakers from the peasant activist group, which had been shut out of February's consultation meetings, called the summit a "sham exercise" while others questioned why recommendations from the consultation were completely absent from the summit agenda.

Not only that, but participants also asked FAO staff where the findings of the FAO convened International Assessment of Agricultural Knowledge, Science and Technology for Development (IAASTD) had gone. That report, which recommended support for small-scale agriculture and attacked biofuels and intellectual property rights, was similarly absent from the summit agenda.

As Mulvany put it, the feeling was that the whole consultation was "a token exercise so that [the FAO and World Bank] could say that there was a consultation with civil society."

At the summit itself, civil society representatives were dismayed to discover that they alone would be forced to enter via the venue's rear entrance. Once inside, they were permitted only a 90-minute forum with an agenda set by the FAO. Meanwhile, according to Mulvany, a private sector round-table upstairs was to be addressed by Kofi Annan, the FAO's head Jaques Diouf and representatives of agribusiness giants like Monsanto and Syngenta.

Other attendants saw the summit as a stage for leaders to use to enhance their images. Helena Paul, head of UK based not for profit Econexus, told me that "The summit has become [an] 'Important' . . . chance for leaders to come to make their pronouncements." While the leaders strutted, Paul told me, and aid pledges trickled in, "pledges are not going to address the underlying crisis. They cannot address the problems of monoculture and industrial agriculture."

A New Greed Revolution?

As the summit unfolded, it became clear that the agenda on display was not geared towards revitalizing local agriculture, protecting biodiversity, the health of consumers and the planet's atmosphere. Instead of focusing on making trade fairer, restoring seed and grain banks, setting up marketing boards for local produce, agreeing to a moratorium on biofuel cultivation, supporting land reform efforts and setting up institutions to spread the accumulated knowledge of indigenous cultivators, the summit declaration called for more production and higher yields. Instead of recognizing the systemic failures of the global market, it was decided that better technology and investment could allow farmers to produce humanity out of its nutritional crisis.

What the [United Nations] summit in Rome was really all about was opening up the political space to sweep away regulations and to pry open already gaping markets.

As UN Secretary General Ban Ki Moon wrote in an editorial as the summit opened, "What's needed, in effect, is a second green revolution of the sort than once transformed southeast Asia" while "there is no reason why productivity cannot be doubled within a relatively short span, easing scarcity worldwide." Ban's predecessor, Kofi Annan (now chairman of the corporate-funded Alliance for a New Green Revolution in Africa) told the summit that "We hope to spur a green revolution in Africa which respects biodiversity and the continent's distinct regions."

The end of summit declaration made increased production its center-piece, but it also promised increased investment in "science and technology for food and agriculture" a blanket term which could include support for genetic modification, leaving the door wide open for a new, genetic, Green Revolution to sweep the developing world.

The emphasis throughout the summit was on liberalization and deregulation. Despite the rhetoric about new "revolutions" to feed the world, what the FAO summit in Rome was really all about was opening up the political space to sweep away regulations and to pry open already gaping markets even further. GRAIN's Henk Hobbelink told me that "The outcome of the Summit is even worse than what we feared." While "the governments did not even manage to agree to stop the disastrous advance of agrofuels [and] where they did agree, many of the proposed measures go exactly in the wrong direction: more market liberalisation, more high tech solutions, more freedom [for] corporations and more chemicals."

Food sovereignty campaigners came out of the summit frustrated. As Herman Kumara, of Via Campesina and the World Forum of Fisher Peoples put it, "The claims of social movements for more protection and support for sustainable and small scale food producers, for comprehensive Land and Agrarian Reforms and concrete measures against financial speculation have been totally ignored by the governments [at the summit]." Activist Flavio Valente of FIAN International commented that "It is disappointing, that the governments still do not recognize that the present food crisis is the result of decades of structural adjustment that have systematically violated the right to food."

Downhill All the Way from the Summit

Developments since the summit have closely followed what U.S. representatives in Rome called its "three prong strategy" to deal with the food crisis, while further marginalizing advocates of food sovereignty and small farmers.

U.S. Agriculture Secretary Ed Schafer, representing the [President George W.] Bush administration, told reporters in Rome that "first, the president has committed an immediate and expanded humanitarian response." Secondly, he said that "Longstanding issues of improving agriculture productivity, alleviating market bottlenecks and promoting market-based principles remain and therefore require immediate attention," making liberalization of global markets a key element of the strategy. Finally, Schafer concluded that "we ask all countries to allow the free flow of food and the safe technologies that produce that food."

The nature of this "safe technology" was made crystal clear, as Schafer continued, commenting that "certainly we think that GMOs (genetically modified organisms) are safe. We've been using them for 10 years in the United States and they have a proven effectiveness in increasing yields, in lowering the use of fertilizer, in providing better water and soil management and also increasing taste and appearance. So, you know, those are all good things."

Biotech firms are looking to thrive in the context of rising food prices.

Investment capital, agri-giants like-Cargill, biotech firms (principally Monsanto) and the U.S. and European governments are marching in step with this strategy. A push to expand GMO cultivation and remove protections for local agriculture is clearly underway, and there is a massive amount of money at stake.

As the *Financial Times* put it in a . . . report on Monsanto's third quarter earnings, announced in late June [2008], "Shares in the St Louis-based company have more than doubled in the past year as investors bet that spikes in crop prices and rising demand for food in the developing world would sustain strong markets both for seeds and for Monsanto's Roundup herbicide."

Biotech firms are looking to thrive in the context of rising food prices. Few evince this better than Thomas West, a director of biotech affairs with Dupont, who told *Reuters* that "It is critical we keep moving forward . . . We have to yield and produce our way out of this." At the same biotech conference, Syngenta's executive industry relations head director Jack Bernens said that "You can bring a number of tools to bear with biotechnology to solve problems . . . As food prices increase . . . it certainly brings a more practical perspective to the debate."

The Supposed Biotech Saviors

However, a few voices have been more circumspect. *The Guardian* disclosed . . . that Syngenta chairman Martin Taylor told an audience at a recent conference that "GM won't solve the food crisis, at least not in the short term," citing a lack of crop varieties adapted to the climates of developing nations. He also called for the liberalization of regulations to "allow companies to develop thousands of GM crops for smaller, more diverse market"—indicating another strategy being employed by the biotech giants: pose as saviors and then blame government for restraining them from saving the world.

The only difference is that Syngenta sees itself as a savior in the near future. Monsanto wants to save us right now. The difference also reflects the fact that U.S. based Monsanto enjoys few regulations on its testing, while Syngenta—based in Europe—receives much more scrutiny from the EU [European Union] and national governments.

However, this may all be changing. June [2008] saw the announcement of a major EU study and review group to look at the deregulation of GM crops across Europe. Britain's Prime Minister Gordon Brown told reporters that GM could "play an important role in mitigating the effects of the food crisis" while the President of the EU Commission, Jose Manuel Barroso, went further. Barroso said that rising food prices had added what he called a "new dimension" to the debate on GM foods, adding that "The recent surge in agricultural commodity prices could be exacerbated by trade obstacles related to GMOs" and recommending that Europe join the U.S. in embracing biotechnology.

The British government is taking the lead in this shift. Aside from Gordon Brown's comments, one of his lieutenants—Environment Minister Phil Woolas—told the *Independent* newspaper that "There is a growing question of whether GM crops can help the developing world out of the current food price crisis" adding that "It is a question that we as a nation need to ask ourselves."

World agricultural policy is still being drafted to suit the interests of a tiny clique of investors and corporate officials.

The British government and the EU Commission are paving the way for the deregulation of GM crops and food, using the food crisis as cover, evidence that they are fully on board with Washington's "three-prong strategy" to take advantage of rising food prices worldwide.

Indeed, this European drift towards a much more supportive policy on GMOs comes soon after Monsanto announced "a new push to feed the world." Using its privileged position at the FAO summit, Monsanto told gathered officials that it would be adopting "ambitious goals to boost global food production, funnelling millions into public research on wheat and rice . . . while pledging to double yields on corn and soy by 2030 [and pledging to] distribute seeds to African farmers royalty-free" as reported by *Business Week* magazine.

Monsanto's CEO [chief executive officer] Hugh Grant has been candid about his company's position, saying that "[philanthropy] isn't a feel-good thing." For Monsanto, "Satisfying the demand curve is a great business opportunity." Global starvation has produced quite a demand curve, and GMOs are set to "satisfy" it. Despite the fact that drought tolerant, transgenic white corn remains some years off (most transgenic corn is used to produce animal feed) Monsanto is "working with African aid groups to develop" such crops. They are, in other words, putting in the ground work for the mass adoption of GM technology in the near future. . . .

A Monoculture-opoly

World agricultural policy is still being drafted to suit the interests of a tiny clique of investors and corporate officials. According to a recent paper by Food First analysts Eric Holt-Gimenez and Loren Peabody, three companies control the world's grain trade: Cargill, Archer Daniels Midland and Bunge, while Monsanto controls around 60 percent of global seed production. The grain giants benefit from liberalization, allowing them to flood markets with subsidized produce, speculate on cross border currency shifts and source production from immiserated rural proletariats. At the same time, Monsanto benefits from the promotion of GM foods to boost food production, for obvious reasons.

It is the interests of these companies, and the interests that they support (including fertilizer manufacturers, supermarket chains and investment banks) that are being served by the response so far to the global food crisis. A better way of phrasing that may well be the global food *opportunity*, considering the nature of the response, which is precisely what we would expect from disaster capitalism at work.

Small farmers will continue to be swamped by heavily subsidized American and European crops, fall prey to land grabs to service the biofuel industry and become indentured to biotech corporations as the global seed supply becomes ever more consolidated. Biodiversity will continue to suffer assault from pesticides, stray genetic information, monoculture plantations and the search of poor peasants for firewood and food. Carbon emissions from grain shipment, farm equipment and deforestation will not abate. The recipe is, in short, one for catastrophe.

However, at the moment the response to this crisis is in the hands of those who are promoting such a ruinous agenda. It is true that alternative power blocs have arisen to challenge international financial institutions and to push for solutions to the food crisis—as in Latin America. India, the Philippines and Malaysia, meanwhile, have imposed restrictions on grain exports. Biofuels have been firmly knocked off their pedestal and their proponents are now scrambling to designate them as "sustainably produced." Food riots have also terrified global policy makers, while campaigners continue to put the food sovereignty alternative on the political table.

This is, as Mulvany told me, an "interesting conjuncture and an exciting time." There is a window for resistance to scale the walls of the global citadel. As Holt-Gimenez reminds us though, it is also a dangerous time, with governments pleading for "support" from the World Bank and a new wave of corporate enrichment likely to masquerade as charity.

What happened in Rome might not have determined the future of global farming, but it may be a turning point in the fight for a fair, sustainable, bottom-up world of fields, watersheds, forests, grasslands and valleys. We are being told—as Holt-Gimenez puts it—to "ask an arsonist to put out a forest fire." But I know who I'd trust to put our global food system right.

Genetically Modified Crops Do Not Produce Greater Yields

Union of Concerned Scientists

The Union of Concerned Scientists was formed in 1969 as a science-based nonprofit organization to work for a healthy environment and a safer world.

News stories on soaring food prices [in 2008] worldwide have cited unsubstantiated claims that genetically engineered crops are the solution to the problem. In fact, according to experts at the Union of Concerned Scientists (UCS), there is no evidence that currently available genetically engineered crops strengthen drought tolerance or reduce fertilizer use. Nor do they fundamentally increase crop yields.

Biotech Overstates Its Impact on the Food Crisis

"Increased energy prices, harsh weather, and trade policies are largely to blame for the recent spike in food prices, none of which have much to do with crop breeding technologies," said Margaret Mellon, director of UCS's Food and Environment Program. "The biotech industry's claims about genetically altered crops are perennially overstated. In truth, agricultural biotechnology has almost nothing to offer to the world food crisis in the short term.

"Today's high prices, however, do point to a future of increased demand for food, where the choice of plant breeding technologies and production methods will indeed play a large role," she added. "But it remains to be seen if biotech will be a significant part of the solution."

Regardless, [President George W.] Bush administration, biotechnology and agribusiness officials are trumpeting genetically engineered crops—and journalists largely have reported their statements without question. For example, a June 5 [2008] *Los Angeles Times* story on a U.N. [United Nations] emergency food summit reported that "American officials are also using the summit to promote genetic engineering as a way to boost food production by increasing crop yields, creating drought-resistant strains and fighting disease such as stem rust in wheat."

Likewise, on May 14 [2008], a *Chicago Tribune* story quoted Dan Price, identified as a food aid expert on the White House's National Security Council. "We certainly think that it is established fact that a number of bio-engineered crops have shown themselves to increase yields through their drought resistance and pest resistance," Price told the *Tribune*.

Commercially available crops have failed to exhibit the critical traits necessary to produce enough food to feed the world's population.

And, according to a May 20 [2008] *Investor's Business Daily* story, "Soaring world food prices appear to be chipping away at public and commercial objections to GM [genetically modified] crops that sharply raise yields and slash growing costs for corn, wheat and other staples," despite the fact that there is currently now genetically engineered wheat on the market. The story went on to quote the president of the American Farm Bureau Federation, who said, "I think the debate about higher prices and being able to meet the demand of people in the world for food is a perfect opportunity to make the case [for GM crops]."

Genetic Engineering Does Not Increase Crop Yields

Biotechnology firms have been hyping genetically engineered crops for more than a decade. During that time, the commercially available crops have failed to exhibit the critical traits necessary to produce enough food to feed the world's population. Those traits include increases in maximum yields and improved drought and stress tolerance. In reality, most of these crops available today are engineered to withstand the application of glyphosate, a weedkiller. A much smaller portion of these crops are engineered to fight off certain pests. Neither of these traits is vital to increasing food production.

"Let's be clear: there are no crops on the market today genetically engineered to directly maximize yields," said Mellon, a molecular biologist. "There are no crops on the market engineered to resist drought. And there are no crops on the market engineered to reduce fertilizer use. Not one."

There are proven ways to increase yields and protect crops, Mellon pointed out. "Traditional plant breeding, crop rotation and marker-assisted breeding—which incorporates molecular biology to enhance traditional breeding—and ecological farming systems that use such methods as crop rotation and cover crops, have a long history of boosting food crop yields. In places like Africa, fertilizer, better grain storage, and improved roads would be much better and more cost-effective options than expensive, patented, biotechnology seeds that so far offer so little.

"GE [genetically engineered] crops may have a role in helping the world feed itself in the future, but today it is still unproven. It is vital that we not let the overheated sales pitch for genetic engineering obscure the better, if less sexy, tools available to address this critical problem."

CHAPTER 4

How Can the
World Solve the
Current Food Crisis?

Chapter Preface

The effects of the brutal increases in food prices in 2007 and 2008 have been seen in every part of the world. The world's poor have, of course, been hardest hit by the food crisis. In wealthy, industrialized countries most people spend 10 to 20 percent of their income on food, so the increase has been difficult but not immediately devastating. The poor in developing nations often spend more than two thirds of their budget to feed themselves, so even small upswings in cost can have calamitous consequences. Since the onset of the food crisis, many of the poorest people in Africa, Asia, and South America have been forced to cut back drastically on their food intake. Many struggle to survive on a single meal a day, and the World Bank estimates that at least 100 million people have been pushed deeper into poverty by soaring food costs.

The lack of consensus regarding the causes of the food crisis has created a situation in which finding a solution is extremely difficult. Biofuel producers deny that they are to blame, while their critics believe that the use of farmland to grow fuel is at the core of the crisis. India and China, believed by many to be contributing to rising demand of food because of their growing affluence, argue that they are largely self-sufficient and thus have no great impact on food costs. Proponents of free-market capitalism counter critics who say that financial markets have caused the wild swings in costs, insisting that it is not the free market but the mismanagement of governments that have created the global mess.

With so little agreement about the roots of the problem, many calls for change to improve the situation have been met with skepticism and criticism that various measures will only make the situation worse. However, one positive idea that has emerged from the debate about the crisis is that the best way to tackle this problem of such enormous magnitude is with small-scale solutions. Numerous non-governmental agencies have shown that the best way of ensuring lasting food security around the world is not simply with periodic infusions of global aid, but by putting in place structures that allow small local farmers to be given a chance at feeding their communities. The United Nations, in calling for aid for poor countries, has as part of its plan measures to increase the success of small farmers. Food activists have noted that small-scale and sustainable farming practices bring communities together by making food production a common purpose and means of sustaining their populations, rather than a source of economic gain for a wealthy few. And even advocates of biotechnology call for the use of genetically modified seeds to help improve the harvests of poor independent growers.

How to allow small farmers in poor countries to gain this independence is a more difficult question. Nobel Prize-winning economist Mohammad Yunus, who developed the concept of microcredit that has seen great success around the world, says that deep structural changes are needed in order to attain this goal, but they are not out of reach. He calls for continuing emergency food relief so that starving populations do not become devastated, while at the same time investing in technology that will ensure healthy harvests in the future—and reduce, and ultimately eliminate, dependence on this aid. Another key, he believes, is to do away with farm subsidies in wealthy countries, which is a politically sensitive issue but one that is central to the problem. Finally, he thinks that wealthy countries owe the poor in the world some of their wealth, not as mere handouts but as part of a strategy that can help them to build their agriculture infrastructure. Although the program is ambitious, it points out that this urgent problem needs the collaborative efforts of the world, and that global cooperation that sees local efforts as the key to solving the crisis has the best hope of success.

Raising Agricultural Productivity Will Solve the Food Crisis

Graça Machel

Graça Machel is a member of the Africa Progress Panel.

The factors behind the global food crisis may be complex, but its impact is simple in its brutality. The worst affected countries are those which need to import agricultural produce, and the hardest hit people are those who spend the largest proportion of their incomes on food.

It is therefore the poorest people in the poorest countries who are feeling the brunt of this catastrophe. The Food and Agriculture Organisation notes that 21 of the 37 countries worst affected by high food prices are in Africa, including four of the five countries deemed to be facing "exceptional shortfalls".

[On June 16, 2008] the Africa Progress Panel, on which I sit, produced its inaugural report on the state of Africa, assessing the state of the continent's development and identifying the challenges that threaten progress.

Chaired by Kofi Annan, and including statesmen and women, development experts and high-profile campaigners, the Panel was established to focus world leaders on their commitments to Africa. It has been uncompromising in its assessment and in its demands.

Measures to Tackle the Crisis

The report calls for immediate measures to tackle the current food crisis. The supply of food must be increased by raising the level of financial assistance to the governments of affected countries and aid agencies. All countries must make every effort to increase the quantity of food on international markets, so that the World Food Programme, relief organisations, and individual governments are able to purchase food.

If the scale of the emergency is not acknowledged, or the response to it is delayed, then we will see an increase in hunger and malnutrition. The cost of food wilt not only be measured in the price of wheat or rice, but also in the rising number of infant and child deaths across Africa.

What gives this call to action added resonance is the fact that the African continent over the last few years has been making real, tangible progress. Gross domestic product per capita across Africa has risen steadily since 1994.

According to the most recent estimates of the International Monetary Fund, the rate of growth reached 6.6% in 2007, exceeding the Middle East and Latin America. The number of people living in poverty has leveled off over the past few years, and Africa's poverty rate has declined by almost 6 percentage points since 2000. There have also been significant improvements in health and education.

We must ... raise agricultural productivity ... [by] reforming outdated policies and investing in ... fertilizer, improved seeds, effective water management and new crop varieties.

Primary school enrollment has increased 36 percentage points between 1999 and 2005, and infant and child mortality have declined in many parts of the continent. These hard-fought gains are now at risk. The Panel's report shows that the food crisis threatens to destroy years, if not decades, of economic progress in Africa.

100 million people could be pushed back into absolute poverty. For me, this is where the real tragedy lies. The very people who have fought against the odds, harnessed their tal-

ents to better their lives, and dared hope that their children will continue the journey, could see their efforts reduced to nothing.

It is the ability of these people in particular to have a stake in their economies that will, I believe, determine the future prosperity and security of our continent. The Panel is therefore calling for more than immediate outside assistance to alleviate the problems of high food prices. As Africans we must take responsibility for the fundamental, structural problems with agricultural productivity on our continent.

The Need for New Agricultural Methods

With the lowest use of fertilizers in the world, average grain yield in Africa is less than one ton per hectare, equivalent to just one quarter of the global average. Our population has increased, yet African agricultural yields have stagnated since the early 1960s. We must therefore raise agricultural productivity and increase food production.

This includes reforming outdated policies and investing in key inputs such as fertilizer, improved seeds, effective water management and new crop varieties, and linking farmers to markets via investments in basic infrastructure. In short, Africa needs a green revolution. If the challenge seems daunting, then there is some comfort in knowing that the expertise and the experience exist.

With appropriate technology and support, for example, Malawi has gone from experiencing serious food shortages to becoming both self-reliant and a net exporter of food. The key is to build on this success and replicate it across the continent.

It is no co-incidence that the Africa Progress Panel has published its report just a few days ahead of the [2008] European Council Summit in Brussels and a few weeks ahead of the G8 [Group of 8] Summit in Hokkaido, Japan. Our report shows that, despite progress on debt relief and significant increases in assistance by individual countries, the G8's [an international forum for 8 influential governments] commitments to double assistance to Africa by 2010—agreed at Gleneagles in 2005—are badly off-track.

With a shortfall of US$40 billion in aid, G8 countries must urgently address the deficits against their targets, set clear timetables for delivery and increase transparency in order to improve the quality of aid. The food crisis has put a clear premium on the G8 delivering its original pledges.

I am conscious that on numerous occasions in the last few decades, it has been said that Africa is at a cross-roads. If we agree that the continent has demonstrated real progress in the last decade, and we acknowledge that the food crisis threatens to reverse much of this, then we are—once again—at a defining moment.

European and G8 leaders should be in no doubt when they gather in Brussels and Hokkaido that they face a very real test of leadership. Many millions of people across the world—and no more so than in Africa—are demanding that they deliver.

Combining Traditional Methods and New Technologies Will Improve Farming

M.S. Swaminathan

Professor M.S. Swaminathan is a member of the Parliament of India and the former Chairman of the National Commission on Farmers.

A high-level conference on World Food Security has been convened by the Food and Agriculture Organisation of the United Nations (FAO) in Rome from June 3–5, 2008. The conference is in response to the growing global food emergency arising partly from the steep escalation in the price of fossil fuels and partly from weather aberrations. The conference will consider both the pressing problems of today and the emerging problems arising from climate change and diversion of prime farmland for the production of bioenergy.

It has become a trend in such conferences for heads of governments/states from Africa and other developing countries to participate in large numbers. In contrast, the industrialised countries tend to be represented either by their ambassadors in Rome or senior officials. It has also become customary in such large international political gatherings for developing countries to blame both rich countries and the WTO [World Trade Organisation] for not responding to their needs adequately and at the right time. The industrialised countries, in turn, stress that developing countries normally neglect their farmers and also exhibit a deficit in governance and surplus in corruption. At the end of the meeting, a few small gestures of immediate assistance will be forthcoming along with volumes of advice, but the long-term problems will remain under the carpet. The entire exercise, involving considerable expenditure, ultimately becomes a forum for photo opportunity and media cynicism. The poor nations and the poor in all nations will suffer most from the inaction associated with such a blame game.

The Right to Food

As the immediate past president of the Pugwash Conference on Science and World Affairs, I wish to quote what Bertrand Russell and Albert Einstein said in a Manifesto issued on 5 April 1955: "We appeal as human beings, to human beings. Remember your humanity and forget the rest. If you can do so, the way lies open to a new Paradise, if you cannot, there lies before you the risk of universal death."

This immortal appeal is the guiding principle behind the Pugwash movement for a nuclear-peril free world. An even greater peril confronting us today is the spectre of widespread hunger and the consequent food riots. Unless the right to food becomes a fundamental human right and gets enforced legally and socially, the hungry will have to eat only promises and platitudes.

The answer ... lies in improving the productivity and profitability of major farming systems in an environmentally sustainable manner.

Reducing hunger and poverty by half by 2015 is the first among the U.N. [United Nations] Millennium Development Goals which, in my view, represent a Global Common Minimum Programme for Sustainable Human Security and Peace. Unfortunately, an assessment made at the end of five years of the 15-year period revealed that most developing countries, including India, are not making proportionate advance in achieving even this very modest target. China is a notable exception to this trend. There are no technical, economic or political excuses for the failure to eliminate endemic hunger in an effective manner. This is unfortunate since food occupies the first position among the hierarchical needs of a human being. This is why Roman philosopher Seneca mentioned over 2000 years ago that a hungry person listens neither to religion nor reason nor is bent by any prayer. The widespread social unrest we see today in many parts of the world is partly due to the growing rich-poor divide in entitlement to the minimum purchasing power essential for household nutrition security.

Threats to Human Security

Compounding the problems arising from poverty and unemployment are the new threats to human security arising from the rising cost of petroleum products and the consequent diversion of land and crops for fuel and feed production. The answer to these questions lies in improving the productivity and profitability of major farming systems in an environmentally sustainable manner. In most developing countries affected by high food prices, agriculture is the main source of rural livelihoods. They should hence initiate steps to take advantage of the vast untapped production reservoir existing with the technologies on the shelf, and thereby build a sustainable food security system based on home grown food. For example, in Africa, Asia and Latin America, the average yield of food crops like sorghum, maize, millets and grain legumes is less than 50 per cent of what can be achieved. Most of the farms in the developing countries of Asia are small in size, often less than two hectares. The smaller the farm the greater is the need for marketable surplus in order to get some cash income. Carefully planned agricultural progress can help to create simultaneously more food, income and jobs. It is only agriculture, including crop and animal husbandry, fisheries, forestry and agro-processing that can promote job-led economic growth. Modern industry, in contrast, promotes jobless growth, which will lead to joyless growth in population rich nations.

Besides responding to the immediate food needs, the global community should help nations affected by the food crisis in the following areas:

- Help to launch a *Bridge the Yield Gap Movement* in order to close the gap between potential and actual yields in the major food and feed crops through mutually reinforcing technologies, services and public policies.

- Strengthen the rural infrastructure particularly in the area of post-harvest technology including processing, storage, value-addition and marketing.

- Give the highest priority to providing small farm families with opportunities for assured and remunerative marketing at the time of harvest; small farmers are more concerned with present trading than futures' trading.

- Ensure that the ongoing Doha Round of Negotiations in WTO results in methods of promoting *free and fair* trade. This will involve cutting down of heavy farm subsidies by industrialised nations and providing more income earning opportunities for developing countries through trade.

The Effective Cooperation of Tradition and Modernity

The agriculture of industrialised nations is energy intensive, while most of the traditional agricultural practices in developing countries are knowledge intensive. Therefore, developing nations should not take to the path of energy intensive agronomic practices but should refine the traditional methods of soil health enhancement and pest management and blend them with modern technology. Also, developing nations should fully harness their vast animal wealth. India for example, has over 20 per cent of the world's cattle, buffalo, sheep and goat populations. It will therefore be prudent to promote crop-livestock integrated farming systems, rather than monoculture of the same crop and variety. In other words, the global energy and food crises have opened up uncommon opportunities for developing nations to promote conservation farming and sustainable rural livelihoods. This will help them to achieve an evergreen revolution leading to the improvement of productivity in perpetuity without associated ecological harm. Population rich, but land hungry countries like India, China and Bangladesh, have no option except to produce more per units of land and water under conditions of diminishing per capita arable land and irrigation water availability, and expanding biotic and abiotic stresses.

While participation in large high-profile international conferences may be important politically, charity begins at home and we must first attend to our own hungry who constitute the bulk of the hungry in Asia. Our immediate tasks are first to enable the over 4 crore [Hindu unit of value equal to ten million rupees] of farmers relieved from the debt trap as a result of loan waivers to restart their agriculture in an effective manner and, secondly, to assist all farmers in the country to derive maximum benefit from the normal southwest monsoon which has arrived in Kerala. A *good weather code* will involve attention to all links in the production, consumption and commerce-chain. The necessary inputs, particularly seeds of appropriate varieties and the nutrients essential for balanced fertilization, should be available at the right time and place and at affordable prices. The extension effort should focus on the adoption of risk-minimising and soil enriching technologies. The minimum support price should be announced at the time of sowing and a remunerative procurement price offered at the time of harvest based on national and international market prices.

Drought and Flood Codes

In addition to a good weather code, *drought and flood codes* should also be kept ready. The drought code will involve the popularisation of crop life-saving techniques and the cultivation of low water-requiring but high-value crops like pulses and oilseeds. Tuber crops will also do well even if planted somewhat late. The flood code should have strategies ready for post-flood farming activities. Seeds and planting material of alternative crops should be built up. After floods, the aquifer will contain adequate water and it is important that the post-flood season becomes a remunerative cropping season. Contingency plans for the flood prone plains of Uttar Pradesh, Bihar and Assam involving alternative cropping strategies should be prepared forthwith.

With a population of over 1.1 billion, India's agricultural strategy should aim to keep the Central and State governments in a commanding position with reference to the management of food distribution systems such as PDS [Public Distribution System], ICDS [Integrated Child Development Services], and school noon meal programme. In the ultimate analysis, assured and remunerative marketing will hold the key to stimulate and sustain farmers' interest in producing for the market. Climate change may result in adverse changes in temperature, precipitation and sea level. Dependence only on wheat and rice will enhance vulnerability to climatic factors. Therefore, there should be revitalisation of the earlier food traditions of rural and tribal families, who in the past depended for their daily bread on a wide range of millets, grain legumes, tubers and vegetables. The PDS should include, wherever appropriate, ragi and a wide range of nutritious cereals, inappropriately referred to as coarse cereals, and tubers.

India has the technological and economic capability to demonstrate how farming systems can be adjusted to different weather patterns. It is hoped that at the Rome Conference, Indian representatives will serve as a bright affirming flame in the midst of the sea of despair we see around us. In this hour of grave energy and food crises, we should revert to the advice of Russell and Einstein and remember our humanity and forget everything else. The call for "Food for All" which will be made by world leaders in Rome on June 3, 2008 will not then remain a populist slogan.

America's Agricultural Policies Must Be Changed

Terra Lawson-Remer

Terra Lawson-Remer teaches Institutions & Economic Development at New York University.

[In late May 2008] Congress passed a pork laden farm bill that could cost American taxpayers up to $289 billion over five years. At the same time, a global food crisis is deepening. Average prices for wheat, rice, and corn have gone up 41 percent since October 2007. Food riots are rocking cities from Haiti to Egypt to Ethiopia. Tragically, U.S. agricultural policies, designed to placate American agribusiness, are contributing significantly to today's global food crisis.

In the short-term, skyrocketing food prices have been driven by a perfect storm of rising reliance on biofuels; droughts and floods in key food producing regions; the surging price of oil, which raises the costs of petrochemical fertilizers and transportation; and rising demand for meat in China and other newly prosperous areas of the developing world.

According to the International Food Policy Research Institute, 30% of the U.S. maize crop currently goes to ethanol production, and biofuel subsidies range between US$11 billion and US$13 billion a year. By encouraging U.S. farmers to switch land away from food production, U.S. subsidies for ethanol contribute to the biofuel dimension of the food crisis.

The Effects of American Subsidies Abroad

In the long-term though, the real damage done by America's agricultural policies has been to undermine agriculture in developing countries. This structural imbalance makes poor countries reliant on food imports and vulnerable to volatile international food markets; limits opportunities for agriculture exports; decreases global food supply; and prevents farmers in poor countries from quickly growing more food in response to rising demand.

Since [World War II], U.S. farm policies have promoted the growth of agribusiness by guaranteeing prices to assure profitability as well as paying farmers not to grow in order to prevent a glut of food on the market. Developing country farmers simply cannot compete—domestically or internationally—with cheap subsidized rice, corn, and wheat from the United States. This market distortion undermines both public and private investment in food production in the global south.

When Peru introduced a "shock" import liberalization program in the 1990s to lower tariffs, food imports increased dramatically, particularly of cereals and rice. According to Oxfam International, increased food imports stiffened the market competition faced by smallholder farmers, who cultivate traditional Andean products like quinoa and potatoes. The availability of cheap, imported grain changed eating patterns in favor of wheat and rice, and precipitated a decline in potato consumption.

Cheap food from the U.S. reduces the incentive for developing country governments and the international development community to invest in increasing the productivity of small hold farmers in Africa, because even more productive crops would be competing against subsidized U.S. food exports. The green revolution of the 1960s in Asia—an important underpinning of subsequent economic growth—was spurred by advances in agricultural productivity targeted towards the soil, climate, and crops specific to the region. Farm yields doubled and tripled within a decade. Similar technological investments have not been made in African agriculture. In fact, public agricultural research and development spending actually declined during the 1990s. African farmers lack access to improved seeds and fertilizer, and many small producers grow less than one-fifth as much on the same amount of land as their counterparts in Asia.

Artificially cheap global food prices over the past few decades, made possible by U.S. agricultural subsidies, are making the world's poor vulnerable to skyrocketing food prices today.

The inability to compete with subsidized U.S. crops also reduces the incentive for governments to invest in the rural-to-urban transportation infrastructure urgently needed by farmers. Currently, poor transport infrastructure makes it very costly for rural farmers to export crops or get their goods to domestic urban centers. But even if transport costs were decreased significantly, the reductions might not be sufficient to overcome the subsidy advantage enjoyed by American agribusiness.

Moreover, competition from cheap U.S. food imports have encouraged some rural farmers to focus on subsistence farming or to abandon farming entirely and move to cities. At the same time, U.S. subsidies make it more difficult for food exporters to find buyers on the international market. Competition from U.S. subsidized agribusiness—both domestically and internationally—has shrunk agricultural capacity in developing countries, making it difficult for farmers to quickly grow more food now in response to rising prices.

The demand of a growing urban workforce for affordable food has historically played a key role in pushing governments and farmers to make food cheaper by boosting agricultural yields and reduce production costs. When urban food demand is met by subsidized food imports, there is less pressure for farmers to produce more, or for governments to improve agricultural productivity or transportation infrastructure so rural farmers can get their crops to cities. Being priced out of the international market depresses public and private investments even more. In a vicious circle, underinvestment contracts the agricultural sector, makes small hold farmers less competitive, and increases the price of food grown in developing countries compared to subsidized crops from the United States.

Ironically, artificially cheap global food prices over the past few decades, made possible by U.S. agricultural subsidies, are making the world's poor vulnerable to skyrocketing food prices today.

The Problem with Food Aid

At the same time, U.S. food "aid" is more a vehicle to dump excess U.S. production than a benefit for hungry populations. Congress requires that food aid be purchased from U.S. growers and shipped overseas. This hurts developing country farmers by undercutting them in their local markets, further reducing domestic production. The policy also prevents the U.S. from contributing to the emergence of food futures markets in the global south. Lack of predictability often makes poor farmers reluctant to invest in improvements that may not turn a profit for several years. Futures contracts, common in the U.S. and Europe but virtually unheard of in rural Africa, Asia, or Latin America, would guarantee farmers' incomes and increase incentives to make investments with short-term costs but long-term gains.

Meeting the growing demand for food in the face of rising energy costs requires increasing the agricultural productivity of small-hold staple food farmers in Africa and the Caribbean; reducing reliance on oil dependent inputs like petrochemical fertilizer; improving the transport infrastructure necessary for developing country farmers to be competitive; and raising the profits realized by small farmers in poor countries, in order to encourage them to produce more. Key is improving agricultural yields using techniques other than oil based petrochemicals. These measures will reduce poor countries' reliance on volatile international oil and food markets and increase global food supply.

A long term solution to the food crisis is very difficult so long as U.S. agricultural policies continue to distort the market. The real tragedy of the global food crisis is that the hunger gripping families from Port-au-Prince, Haiti to Yaounde, Cameroon is not inevitable. The blame rests, at least in part, with us.

Water Scarcity Must Be Addressed to Solve the Food Crisis

Fred Pearce

Fred Pearce is a journalist based in the United Kingdom. He is the environment consultant for New Scientist *magazine and has written several books on climate change.*

After decades in the doldrums, food prices have been soaring this year, causing more misery for the world's poor than any credit crunch. The geopolitical shockwaves have spread round the world, with food riots in Haiti, strikes over rice shortages in Bangladesh, tortilla wars in Mexico, and protests over bread prices in Egypt.

The immediate cause is declining grain stocks, which have encouraged speculators, hoarders, and panic-buyers. But what are the underlying trends that have sown the seeds for this perfect food storm?

Biofuels are part of it, clearly. A quarter of U.S. corn is now converted to ethanol, powering vehicles rather than filling stomachs or fattening livestock. And the rising oil prices that encouraged the biofuels boom are also raising food prices by making fertilizer, pesticides, and transport more expensive.

But there is something else going on that has hardly been mentioned, and that some believe is the great slow-burning, and hopelessly underreported, resource crisis of the 21st century: water.

Climate change, overconsumption and the alarmingly inefficient use of this most basic raw material are all to blame. I wrote a book three years ago titled *When The Rivers Run Dry*. It probed why the Yellow River in China, the Rio Grande and

Colorado in the United States, the Nile in Egypt, the Indus in Pakistan, the Amu Darya in Central Asia, and many others are all running on empty. The confident blue lines in a million atlases simply do not tell the truth about rivers sucked dry, for the most part, to irrigate food crops.

We are using these rivers to death. And we are also pumping out underground water reserves almost everywhere in the world. With two-thirds of the water abstracted from nature going to irrigate crops—a figure that rises above 90 percent in many arid countries—water shortages equal food shortages.

Consider the two underlying causes of the current crisis over world food prices: falling supplies from some of the major agricultural regions that supply world markets, and rising demand in booming economies like China and India.

Why falling supplies? Farm yields per hectare have been stagnating in many countries for a while now. The green revolution that caused yields to soar 20 years ago may be faltering. But the immediate trigger, according to most analysts, has been droughts, particularly in Australia, one of the world's largest grain exporters, but also in some other major suppliers, like Ukraine. Australia's wheat exports were 60 percent down last year; its rice exports were 90 percent down.

Why rising demand? China has received most of the blame here—its growing wealth is certainly raising demand, especially as richer citizens eat more meat. But China traditionally has always fed itself—what's different now is that the world's most populous country is no longer able to produce all its own food.

Water tables are plunging, and in many places water supplies are giving out.

A few years ago, the American agronomist and environmentalist Lester Brown wrote a book called *Who Will Feed China?: Wake Up Call for a Small Planet.* It predicted just this.

China can no longer feed itself largely because demand is rising sharply at a time when every last drop of water in the north of the country, its major breadbasket, is already taken. The Yellow River, which drains most of the region, now rarely reaches the sea, except for the short monsoon season.

Some press reports have recently suggested that China is being sucked dry to provide water for the Beijing Olympics. Would that it were so simple. The Olympics will require only trivial amounts of water. China's water shortages are deep-seated, escalating, and tied to agriculture. Even hugely expensive plans to bring water from the wetter south to the arid north will only provide marginal relief.

A map of world food trade increasingly looks like a map of the water haves and have-nots.

The same is true of India, the world's second most populous country. Forty years ago, India was a basket case. Millions died in famines. The green revolution then turned India into a food exporter. Its neighbor Bangladesh came to rely on India for rice. But Indian food production has stagnated recently, even as demand from richer residents has soared. And the main reason is water.

With river water fully used, Indian farmers have been trying to increase supplies by tapping underground reserves. In the last 15 years, they have bought a staggering 20 million Yamaha pumps to suck water from beneath their fields. Tushaar Shah, director of the International Water Management Institute's groundwater research station in Gujarat, estimates those farmers are pumping annually to the surface 100 cubic kilometers more water than the monsoon rains replace. Water tables are plunging, and in many places water supplies are giving out.

"We are living hand-to-mouth," says D.P. Singh, president of the All India Grain Exporters Association, who blames water shortages for faltering grain production. Last year India began to import rice, notably from Australia. This year, it stopped supplying its densely populated neighbor Bangladesh, triggering a crisis there too.

More and more countries are up against the limits of food production because they are up against the limits of water supply. Most of the Middle East reached this point years ago. In Egypt, where bread riots occurred this spring, the Nile River no longer reaches the sea because all its water is taken for irrigation.

A map of world food trade increasingly looks like a map of the water haves and have-nots, because in recent years the global food trade has become almost a proxy trade in water—or rather, the water needed to grow food. "Virtual water," some economists call it. The trade has kept the hungry in dry lands fed. But now that system is breaking down, because there are too many buyers and not enough sellers.

According to estimates by UNESCO's hydrology institute, the world's largest net supplier of virtual water until recently was Australia. It exported a staggering 70 cubic kilometers of water a year in the form of crops, mainly food. With the Murray-Darling Basin, Australia's main farming zone, virtually dry for the past two years, that figure has been cut in half.

The largest gross exporter of virtual water is the United States, but its exports have also slumped as corn is diverted to domestic biofuels, and because of continuing drought in the American West.

The current water shortages should not mark an absolute limit to food production around the world. But it should do three things. It should encourage a rethinking of biofuels, which are themselves major water guzzlers. It should prompt an expanding trade in food exported from countries that remain in water surplus, such as Brazil. And it should trigger much greater efforts everywhere to use water more efficiently.

On a trip to Australia in the midst of the 2006 drought, I was staggered to see that farmers even in the most arid areas still irrigate their fields mostly by flooding them. Until the water runs out, that is. Few have adopted much more efficient drip irrigation systems, where water is delivered down pipes and discharged close to roots. And, while many farmers are expert at collecting any rain that falls on their land, they sometimes allow half of that water to evaporate from the surfaces of their farm reservoirs.

For too long, we have seen water as a cheap and unlimited resource. Those days are coming to an end—not just in dry places, but everywhere. For if the current world food crisis shows anything, it is that in an era of global trade in "virtual water," local water shortages can reverberate throughout the world—creating higher food prices and food shortages everywhere.

Soil Conditions Must Be Improved to Solve the Food Crisis

Seth Borenstein

Seth Borenstein is an Associated Press science reporter.

Science has provided the souped-up seeds to feed the world, through biotechnology and old-fashioned crossbreeding. Now the problem is the dirt they're planted in.

As seeds get better, much of the world's soil is getting worse and people are going hungry. Scientists say if they can get the world out of the economically triggered global food crisis, better dirt will be at the root of the solution.

Soils around the world are deteriorating with about one-fifth of the world's cropland considered degraded in some manner. The poor quality has cut production by about one-sixth, according to a World Resources Institute study. Some scientists consider it a slow-motion disaster.

In sub-Saharan Africa, nearly 1 million square miles of cropland have shown a "consistent significant decline," according to a March 2008 report by a worldwide consortium of agricultural institutions.

The cause of the current global food crisis is mostly based on market forces, speculation and hoarding, experts say. But beyond the economics lie droughts and floods, plant diseases and pests, and all too often, poor soil.

[In the 1970s and 1980s] through better types of plants, Earth's food production exploded in what was then called the "green revolution." Some people thought the problem of feed ing the world was solved and moved on. However, developing these new "magic seeds" was the easy part. The crucial element, fertile soil, was missing.

The Need to Improve Soil

"The first thing to do is to have good soil," said Hans Herren, winner of the World Food Prize. "Even the best seeds can't do anything in sand and gravel."

Herren is co-chairman of the International Assessment of Agricultural Knowledge, Science and Technology for Development, a collection of scientists sponsored by the United Nations and World Bank. It produced a 2,500-page report [April 2008] . . . which, among other recommendations, emphasized a need to improve the world's soil.

Genetic improvements in corn make it possible to grow up to 9,000 pounds of corn per acre in Africa. But millions of poor African farmers only get about 500 pounds an acre "because over the years, their soils have become very infertile and they can't afford to purchase fertilizers," said Roger Leakey, a co-author of the international report and professor at James Cooke University in Australia.

Fixing soil just isn't "sexy" enough to interest governments or charities.

Soil and water issues "have been taken for granted," said Ohio State University soil scientist Rattan Lal. "It is a problem that is not going to be solved. It's going to get worse before it gets better."

In Africa, farmers are forced to use practices that rob nutrients from the soil, not put it back, said Herren, who heads an Arlington, Va., nonprofit. Fertilizer is a quick, short-term fix, but even that isn't being done, he said.

The current crisis could have been avoided "if we, the world, had promoted fertilizer in Africa and we have known for ages it works," said Pedro Sanchez, Columbia University tropical agricultural director.

The Failure of Agriculture Science

In that way, the problem with soil is a prime example of a larger failing of agriculture science, said Sanchez, who has won both the World Food Prize and a MacArthur genius grant. Scientists have the knowledge to feed the world right now, but that is not happening, Sanchez said. "It's very frustrating, especially when you see children dying."

The fruits of biotechnology and the staples of modern agricultural scientific techniques include irrigation, crop rotation, reduced tilling, use of fertilizer and improved seeds. It's a way of farming differently instead of just using better seeds that requires extra money up-front that many African farmers don't have, scientists said.

Fixing soil just isn't "sexy" enough to interest governments or charities, said Robert Zeigler, director general of the International Rice Research Institute in Manila, Philippines.

Zeigler's center . . . planted its 133rd crop of rice in the same land since 1963, trying to pinpoint the right combination of nitrogen and fertilizer. Better seeds worked wonders. But finding money for soil health is difficult and because of that, less work is accomplished, he said.

The Success of Malawi

But there are success stories, Sanchez said, pointing to the small African country of Malawi. [In 2005] the country's new president invested 8 percent of Malawi's national budget in a subsidy program to get fertilizer and better seeds to small farmers. Each farmer got two bags of fertilizer and 4[frac12] pounds of seeds at less than half the cost.

Before the program started, one-third of Malawi was on food aid and the country wasn't growing enough food for itself, Sanchez said. It was producing 1.2 million tons of maize in 2005. In 2006, Malawi had more than doubled its production. By 2007 and 2008, the crop was up to 3.4 and 3.3 million tons. Now Malawi is exporting corn.

"In two years, the country has changed from a food aid recipient to a food aid donor and is self-sufficient," Sanchez said. "If Malawi can do it, richer countries like Nigeria, Kenya can do it."

Reduced Meat Consumption in the West Will Help Ease the Food Crisis

Raj Patel

Raj Patel, the author of Stuffed and Starved, *is a researcher at the University of KwaZulu-Natal in South Africa and a visiting scholar at the Center for African Studies at the University of California at Berkeley.*

America is the most overweight country on earth. Only three out of 10 Americans have a normal body weight. I should have guessed that one of the side effects of moving to the US would be bloating.

Since leaving London for America a decade ago, [in the late 1990s] I've put on a couple of stone. It's easy enough to blame the food environment here. This is, after all, the land where [President Ronald] Reagan pronounced tomato ketchup a fruit and, more recently, where French fries and chocolate-covered cherries were legally dubbed 'fresh produce' under a US Department of Agriculture (USDA) regulation known as the batter-coating rule.

Meat and Health

I can't just censure America for my condition, of course. Getting older and stopping smoking have accelerated my middle-age spread. I'm more active now than I used to be, but that hasn't kept the podge at bay. And I'm convinced that part of the problem is that I eat meat. I came to America a vegetarian and I've lapsed into occasional chicken and fish (though, because of a residual Hinduism, no beef).

I'm not the only person to be blaming flesh for bad outcomes. In America, meat has been getting some bad press recently. The Humane Society of the United States [in early 2008] posted a widely circulated video, filmed undercover at an abattoir [slaughterhouse] in California. It shows workers ramming cows with fork-lift trucks in order to persuade them to walk. There was a financial incentive for them to do it— 'downer cows', cows that are too sick to walk, are prohibited from entering the food system. By the time the story broke and the USDA announced a recall, most of the beef had already been distributed and fed to children through the school-meal programme.

Even Oprah [Winfrey] has announced that she's going vegan, if only for a three-week 'cleanse'. Oprah has had run-ins with the meat industry before. In 1998, on hearing that American cows were being fed to other American cows in very British BSE-generating practices, she 'stopped cold' her beef consumption. A group of Texas cattlemen were aggrieved. They used one of the handful of legal restrictions to free speech rights in the US: you're not allowed to disparage agricultural products here. They claimed that Oprah had done just that. They lost in court. Twice. Yet the implication, not too far from the surface in Oprah's vegan detox diet, is that there's something fairly toxic about meat.

Meat consumption has come under attack on grounds of ethics, environment and health and has even been blamed for the global food crisis. A couple of weeks back, George [W.] Bush said: 'Worldwide, there is increasing demand. There turns out to be prosperity in the developing world, which is good. . . . So, for example, just as an interesting thought for you, there are 350 million people in India who are classified as middle class. . . . Their middle class is larger than our entire population. And when you start getting wealth, you start demanding better nutrition and better food, and so demand is high, and that causes the price to go up.'

Meat Consumption and the Environment

More people demanding more meat means that more land is dedicated not to growing food for people, but food for animals—up to 9kg of grain for every kilo of beef. Ratcheting up meat consumption will drive up the price of feed grains, other things being equal.

Except that other things aren't equal. Evidence suggests that it's hard to impeach either India or China's meat-eating habits. According to Daryll Ray at the University of Tennessee, the US government's own figures show that China has been a net exporter of meats since 2001, subsidised to some extent by the running down of local grain stores, and an increased import of soybeans. Moreover, it has produced more grain than it has consumed for every year since 2005, and continues to export heavily. When it comes to India, Ray says the story is much the same as China's. In fact India has been a net exporter of grains and meat over nearly all of the past two decades even though it has the world's largest number of hungry people. So the problem is a little deeper than more Indians demanding things, as George Bush claims.

Meat manufacturing is tremendously resource-intensive. . . . [Animals] require water, land and environmental services, all of which they're using unsustainably.

Blaming the world's two most populous countries, India and China, is a bit of misdirection, particularly when the facts point the other way. Although India's chicken consumption has gone from 0.2 million tonnes to 2.3 million [tonnes] today [2008], beef consumption is more or less the same as it was in 1990 and, because of the cultural tilt against it, not forecast to change.

China is certainly the world's largest consumer of meat in aggregate, and that is because it is the world's most populous country. Meat consumption has increased from 24kg per person in 1980 to 54kg [in 2007], and the chief of China operations for Tyson Foods, the world's largest meat packer, predicts that [2008] is the last year that China will be self-sufficient in protein. Against this, soaring prices for meat in China are certainly taking the edge off demand. But until China's meat demand extends its footprint beyond its borders, country number three in terms of global population, the United States, remains a little more obviously culpable. Meat consumption here is rather less sustainable than in China or India. Americans eat an awful lot of meat—around 90kg of meat and fish per person per year.

Within the US, meat manufacturing is tremendously resource-intensive. Partly, this is because there's just so much meat around—nine billion animals per year according to one estimate. They require water, land and environmental services, all of which they're using unsustainably. More than half of American pastures are being over-grazed, and are losing soil at six times their sustainable rate. Water resources are also stretched to breaking point—it takes 100 times more water to produce a kilo of animal than vegetable.

And you've also got the problem of shit. Much of America's cheaper meat is produced on Concentrated Animal-Feeding Operations (CAFO), huge lots on which animals are confined, fed and slaughtered within the same vast facility. These operations produce the equivalent of five tonnes of waste for every US citizen. But the waste isn't regulated in the same way. As researchers in a 2005 Johns Hopkins University study noted, a typical CAFO has about 5,000 animals on it. That number of pigs produces as much waste as a city of 20,000 people, but without any of the plumbing.

At one of the largest lots in the US, at the Harris Cattle Ranch in Coalinga, California, 100,000 cattle are housed on a ranch roughly twice the size of Hyde Park. The waste from these animals is stored in a lagoon of shit bigger than Wembley Stadium. Although such lagoons are meant to be insulated from the rest of the environment, there are reports of effluent leaching into local water supplies. In 1999, Hurricane Floyd caused 50 lagoons to flood in North Carolina, and one lagoon burst its banks, releasing 2 million gallons of soupy red liquid.

The amount of grains fed to US livestock would be enough to feed 840 million people on a plant-based diet.

For CAFO workers, who are some of the poorest in the country, respiratory disease rates are high. And when the waste makes it to the sea, the results are even worse. The run-off is rich in fertilisers. As a result of the run-off in the Mississippi, CAFOs cause an annual 'dead zone' in the Gulf of Mexico the size of New Jersey. And yet CAFOs remain largely untouched by government.

The Effects Around the World

The effects of meat consumption reach beyond America's borders. According to the Food and Agriculture Organisation of the United Nations, nearly a fifth of all greenhouse-gas emissions come from livestock—more than from all forms of transport. Global livestock production is set to double between now and 2050, setting another hurdle on the road to sustainable emissions levels.

A University of Chicago study argued that the average meat eater in the US produces about 1.5 tonnes of CO_2 [carbon dioxide] more than a vegetarian per year. That's because animals are hungry and the grain they eat takes energy, usually fossil fuels, to produce. It takes 2.2 calories of fossil fuel energy to produce a single calorie of plant protein, according to researchers at Cornell University. And lots of that plant protein is required to make animal protein. For chicken, the ratio of energy in to protein out is 4:1. For pork it's 17:1. For lamb, 50:1. For beef, 54:1.

This is a lot of energy, and a lot of grain that gets diverted. The amount of grains fed to US livestock would be enough to feed 840 million people on a plant-based diet. The number of food-insecure people in the world in 2006 was, incidentally, 854 million. Of course, this isn't simply an American phenomenon—in aggregate, rich countries feed about 60 per cent of their grain to livestock.

According to the Union of Concerned Scientists, nearly 70 per cent of antibiotics used in the US are destined to be used on livestock. The meat industry is, understandably, feeling a little defensive. 'It seems the public is getting a terminal case of nutrition whiplash. A study one week contradicts the findings of a study released the previous week and has led to consumers either being downright confused and sceptical, or altogether tuned out from that kind of news reporting,' says Dave Ray from the American Meat Institute. Yet the US diet, high in meat and low in fresh fruits and vegetables, is being increasingly indicted. The Johns Hopkins study argues that it leads to higher rates of heart disease, stroke, cancer and diabetes. The cost associated with poor diet in just these diseases has been estimated at $33 billion per year.

Yet there is enough food to feed the world now and in the future. But not if larger and larger slices of it go to feed animals—a fact that the governments of India, China, and the United States seem unprepared to address.

[In 2008] only about two per cent of Americans are vegans. So the question remains: why is it so hard to go cold tofu? John Cunningham, consumer research manager at the Vegetarian Research Group, has commissioned a series of surveys on meat consumption since the early 1990s, and he has noticed some trends. The number of vegetarians has been going up. Between 2.5 per cent and 10 per cent of Americans are now vegetarian, almost double from a decade before, with numbers of young people higher than the general population. 'There's been a deep change', says Cunningham. 'If you talked about being vegetarian in the 1980s, people were incredulous. Today, people say, "Wow, that's great, I wish I could do that".

More people are finding a way to get there, but me, I'm still stuck. Why do I find it so hard to nudge out the meat from my diet? Well, there's a persistent trend in the data. Vegetarian women outnumber men by two to one. Cunningham notes that there's a connection between meat and masculinity, particularly around beef. 'No one had their manhood questioned for not eating a chicken sandwich,' he says, 'but if you don't eat a hamburger, well . . .'

Giving Up Meat

Bob Torres, author of *Making a Killing*, a study of the philosophy and political economy of veganism, has seen this too. In his job as a professor, he has worked with young men from sports teams. 'Many don't get very far giving up meat—they get all kinds of shit from their team mates, who say things like their athletic performance is going to decline, they're pussies, they're not man enough. And when they find out I'm vegan, some people ask me whether I did it because my wife made me.'

There are other reasons why it's so hard to give up meat. It's certainly harder for working-class Americans to eat sustainably when they are working and living in 'food deserts', those parts of the country where fresh fruit and vegetables are hard to come by, and where processed meats are readily found on convenience-store shelves. But I don't have these excuses. It's entirely possible for me to make the right decision.

And the evidence for me rather tilts against meat consumption. I care about climate change, animal suffering and the condition of people in developing countries. Addressing meat's problems will require a range of policies, from ending the subsidy to meat prices from workers' low wages, to pricing the full cost of meat's pollution into its price, to addressing unsustainable practices in agriculture. But in caring about all this, eating meat is a big strike against my conscience. For this, I can't blame America, China or India. I can only blame myself. It's becoming increasingly clear to me that I'll need to become more human, even if, in America, it means I'm less of a man.

Respect for Women's Rights Is Necessary to Solve the Food Crisis

Yifat Susskind

Yifat Susskind is the communications director for MADRE, an international nonprofit group based in New York that works for women's rights and resources worldwide.

[In June 2008], world leaders are meeting in Rome to devise new strategies for world agriculture. They ought to be promoting women's rights.

The majority of the world's farmers are women. In the poorest countries, where the food crisis is at its worst, women grow and produce 80 percent of all food.

Boosting the capacity of small farmers to produce and sell food locally is a key part of the solution. But as women, many small farmers face gender discrimination that undermines their capacity to feed people.

For example, in many countries, women who grow the food that sustains the majority of the population are not even recognized as farmers. They have no legal right to own land. And women are routinely shut out of government agriculture programs. They lose out on access to credit, seeds, tools and training that is more crucial than ever now, since farmers have to adapt to climate change.

All of this means that policies aiming to resolve the food crisis need also to uphold women's rights.

These policies also must recognize the damage that so-called free trade has caused women.

Failed Policies Have Damaged Women's Livelihoods

Ana Chumba is facing a choice that no mother should ever have to make: whether to feed her daughter or send her to school.

Ana is a small-scale farmer who also sells homemade tortillas to make ends meet. But [in 2008], the cost of staple foods in Nicaragua, where she lives, has more than doubled. If she keeps her daughter out of school to help with the tortillas, they may be able to bring in enough to buy rice, cooking oil and, on a good day, milk.

For most of us, the world food crisis has meant an annoying hike in our grocery bill. For Ana, already living on the brink of survival, it's a true emergency.

Economists explain the food crisis as a perfect storm: rising demand for resource-intensive foods like meat, protracted drought, and more land being used to grow fuel instead of food.

World agriculture policy [should realign] with the interests of small-scale women farmers instead of giant corporations.

But long before biofuels became a household word, international trade rules had bankrupted millions of small farmers in the developing world.

Because of huge government subsidies to factory farms in the United States and Europe, food imported from these countries became cheaper than food produced by local farmers.

As a result, food-producing countries like Nicaragua were turned into food importers, leaving people like Ana at the mercy of global markets.

The global food crisis is no natural disaster. Hunger is a consequence of failed policies.

Fortunately, policies can be changed.

The time to change them is now.

The kind of small-scale, sustainable farming that women traditionally do is exactly the mode of agriculture that we need to expand. The Rome meeting should realign world agriculture policy with the interests of small-scale women farmers instead of giant corporations. If we can do that, we may just be able to meet the challenge of today's global food crisis by feeding all people while protecting the planet.

A Comprehensive Global Plan Is Needed to Solve the Food Crisis

Mohammad Yunus

Mohammad Yunus is a Bangladeshi banker and economist whose successful application of microcredit—the extension of small loans—earned him and his Grameen Bank the Nobel Peace Prize in 2006.

The global food crisis is a dire reality for millions of the world's poor and a major test for the international community. Sustained, generous, wise leadership and broad-based cooperation is required to overcome the crisis and save lives.

Rising food prices have created tremendous pressure in the lives of poor people, for whom basic food can consume as much as two-thirds of their income.

There are many causes of these increasing pressures—oil that costs $120 a barrel; droughts in important producing regions; the increased use of corn for ethanol and soy oil for biodiesel; speculation in commodities markets; and ironically, increased prosperity in large countries such as China, India, Indonesia, and Bangladesh, which make up nearly half the world's population. Continually rising food prices are making it more difficult to feed the poorest of the poor worldwide and will reduce the prospect of achieving many of the [United Nations'] Millennium Development Goals, unless immediate action is taken.

UN [United Nations] Secretary-General Ban Ki-Moon deserves credit for convening the leaders of 27 UN agencies and programs to organize a coordinated response. They have agreed to establish a high-level task force under Ban's leadership, with sound immediate objectives.

A comprehensive global plan should include the following six elements.

Short-Term Relief

First, the international community must rapidly mobilize at least $755m [million], identified by the World Food Programme and UN leaders as necessary for emergency food relief. The Secretary-General might want to mobilize two or three global leaders as special envoys to help the UN find these funds.

Second, we must ensure that farmers are equipped to produce the next harvest. Farmers in many areas cannot afford seeds to plant or natural gas-based fertilizer, whose price has risen along with the price of oil. The International Fund for Agricultural Development is delivering $200m to poor farmers in the most affected countries to boost food production. The Food and Agriculture Organization needs an additional $1.7bn [billion] to help provide seed and fertilizer. The World Bank is doubling its lending for agriculture in Africa over [2008] to $800m and is considering a new rapid financing facility for grant support to especially fragile, poor countries and quicker, more flexible financing for others.

Relative to the size and gravity of the crisis, these sums are very modest and affordable for the international community. In the US alone, high prices have been a boon to farmers and have saved the government billions in crop support payments. The world should respond promptly and generously to help those struggling to survive what the UN calls a "silent tsunami."

Long-Term Goals

Third, beyond these immediate actions, new policies are needed to address the underlying causes of the crisis. Crop subsidies and export controls in many important countries are distorting markets and raising prices; they should be eliminated. In particular, subsidies for ethanol that made sense when oil cost $20 a barrel cannot be justified at $120 a barrel—nor can subsidies for oil. They should be phased out together when the price of oil is above a certain level.

Fourth, the current crisis should not deter the world's search for long-term global solutions to poverty and environmental protection. For example, we should continue efforts to move to second-generation fuels made from waste materials and non-food crops without displacing land used [for] food production. Even the limited amount of biofuels on the market today have been credited with reducing the price of oil, and next-generation fuels can be economically advantageous for poor countries with much less effect on food production. As bad as the impact of high food prices has been, the impact of high oil prices has been worse—devastating poor countries that have no indigenous source of supply, erasing all the benefits of international debt relief and more.

Oil-exporting countries [should] contribute a portion of the greatest wealth transfer the world has ever known to help feed the poor.

Fifth, the world must develop a new system of long-term investments in agriculture. A new "green revolution" is required to meet the global demands, even as climate change is increasing the stresses on agriculture. More productive crops are needed, but also ones that are drought-resistant and salt-tolerant. The Consultative Group on International Agricultural Research must be strengthened to help lead these efforts.

Sixth, to help fund these important initiatives, I propose that each oil-exporting country create a "poverty and agriculture fund", contributing a fixed amount—perhaps 10%—of the price of every barrel of oil exported. This would be a small fraction of the windfall they have been gaining from higher prices. The funds would be managed by the founding nations and devoted to overcoming poverty, improving agricultural yields, supporting research for new technology, and creating social businesses to help solve the problems of the poor, such as health care, education and women's empowerment.

Help from Those Who Have Profited

Just as the US should return a portion of its windfall from grain exports through increased support of food aid, so too should oil-exporting countries contribute a portion of the greatest wealth transfer the world has ever known to help feed the poor.

Thankfully, the Secretary-General and other international leaders are focusing attention on today's crisis, and the world should respond quickly to these calls. But the pressures of a growing and more prosperous population will not go away—demand for food and energy will grow, and the poor will suffer most. The need for long-term investment in agriculture and food aid will grow as well.

Organizations to Contact

The editors have compiled the following list of organizations concerned with the issues debated in this book. The descriptions are derived from materials provided by the organizations. All have publications or information available for interested readers. The list was compiled on the date of publication of the present volume; the information provided here may change. Be aware that many organizations take several weeks or longer to respond to inquiries, so allow as much time as possible.

Center for Global Food Issues
PO Box 202, Churchville, VA   24421
(540) 337-6354 • fax: (540) 337-8593
Web site: www.cgfi.org

The Center for Global Food Issues conducts research and analysis of agriculture and the environmental concerns surrounding food and fiber production. The Center uses its worldwide overview of food and farming to assess policies, improve farmers' understanding of the new globalized farm economy, and heighten awareness of the environmental impacts of various farming systems and food policies. The Center's main goals are to promote free trade in agricultural products for both economic efficiency and environmental conservation; combat efforts to limit technological innovation in agriculture; and heighten awareness of the connection between agricultural productivity and environmental conservation.

Consultative Group on International Agricultural Research (CGIAR)
CGIAR Secretariat, The World Bank, MSN G6-601, 1818 H
   St. NW, Washington, DC   20433
(202) 473-8951 • fax: (202) 473-8110

e-mail: cgiar@cgiar.org
Web site: www.cgiar.org

The Consultative Group on International Agricultural Research, established in 1971, is a strategic partnership, whose 64 members support 15 international centers, working in collaboration with many hundreds of government and civil society organizations as well as private businesses around the world. The CGIAR generates cutting-edge science to foster sustainable agricultural growth that benefits the poor through stronger food security, better human nutrition and health, higher incomes and improved management of natural resources. The results of the CGIAR's collaborative research are made widely available to individuals and organizations working for sustainable agricultural development throughout the world.

GRAIN
Girona 25, pral., Barcelona   E-08010
   Spain
+34 933011381 • fax: +34 933011627
e-mail: grain@grain.org
Web site: www.grain.org

GRAIN is an international non-governmental organization that promotes the sustainable management and use of agricultural biodiversity based on people's control over genetic resources and local knowledge. GRAIN produces several publications, including a quarterly magazine, *Seedling*, and a collection of opinion papers, *Against the Grain*.

Institute for Food and Development Policy/Food First
398 60th St., Oakland, CA   94618
(510) 654-4400 • fax: (510) 654-4551
Web site: www.foodfirst.org

The Institute for Food and Development Policy/Food First shapes how people think by analyzing the root causes of global hunger, poverty, and ecological degradation and developing solutions in partnership with movements working for social change. The purpose of the Institute for Food and Development Policy/Food First is to eliminate the injustices that cause hunger.

International Food Policy Research Institute (IFPRI)
2033 K St. NW, Washington, DC 20006-1002
(202) 862-5600 • fax: (202) 467-4439
e-mail: ifpri@cgiar.org
Web site: www.ifpri.org

The International Food Policy Research Institute seeks sustainable solutions for ending hunger and poverty. IFPRI is one of 15 centers supported by the Consultative Group on International Agricultural Research, an alliance of 64 governments, private foundations, and international and regional organizations. The IFPRI's vision is of a world where every person has secure access to sufficient and safe food to sustain a healthy and productive life and where food-related policy decisions are made transparently and include the participation of consumers and producers.

E.F. Schumacher Society
140 Jug End Rd., Great Barrington, MA 01230
(413) 528-1737 • fax: (413) 528-4472
e-mail: efssociety@smallisbeautiful.org
Web site: www.smallisbeautiful.org

Founded in 1980, the mission of the E.F. Schumacher Society is to promote the building of strong local economies that link people, land, and community. To accomplish this the organization develops model programs, including local currencies, community land trusts, and micro-lending; hosts lectures and other educational events; publishes papers; and maintains a library to engage scholars and inspire citizen-activists.

U.S. Agency for International Development (USAID)
Information Center, Ronald Reagan Building
Washington, DC 20523-1000

(202) 712-4810 • fax: (202) 216-3524
Web site: www.usaid.gov

USAID is the principal U.S. agency extending assistance to countries recovering from disaster, trying to escape poverty, and engaging in democratic reforms. USAID is an independent federal government agency that receives overall foreign policy guidance from the Secretary of State. Its work supports long-term and equitable economic growth and advances U.S. foreign policy objectives by supporting economic growth, agriculture and trade, global health, and conflict prevention and humanitarian assistance.

World Bank
1818 H St. NW, Washington, DC   20433
(202) 473-1000 • fax: (202) 477-6391
Web site: www.worldbank.org

The World Bank is a vital source of financial and technical assistance to developing countries around the world. It is not a bank in the common sense but made up of two development institutions—the International Bank for Reconstruction and Development (IBRD) and the International Development Association (IDA)—owned by 185 member countries. Each institution plays a different but collaborative role to advance the vision of an inclusive and sustainable globalization. The World Bank provides low-interest loans, interest-free credits and grants to developing countries for a wide array of purposes that include investments in education, health, public administration, infrastructure, financial and private sector development, agriculture, and environmental and natural resource management.

World Food Programme (WFP)
Via C.G.Viola 68, Parco dei Medici, Rome   00148
   Italy
+39-06-65131 • fax: +39-06-6513 2840
Web site: www.wfp.org

The World Food Programme, the world's largest humanitarian organization, is the United Nations' frontline agency in the fight against global hunger. WFP pursues a vision of the world in which every man, woman and child has access at all times to the food needed for an active and healthy life. Its food assistance reaches an average of 100 million people in 80 countries every year. Almost 12,000 people work for the organization, most of them in remote areas, directly serving the hungry poor.

Bibliography

Books

Sharon Astyk and Aaron Newton	*A Nation of Farmers: Defeating the Food Crisis on American Soil.* Gabriola Island, British Columbia: New Society Publishers, 2009.
Christopher Cook	*Diet for a Dead Planet: Big Business and the Coming Food Crisis.* New York: New Press, 2006.
Eric Holt-Gimenez and Raj Patel	*Food Rebellions!: Forging Food Sovereignty to Solve the Global Food Crisis.* Oxford, UK: Fahamu Books, 2009.
Naomi Klein	*The Shock Doctrine: The Rise of Disaster Capitalism.* New York: Picador, 2008.
Frances Moore Lappe, Joseph Collins, Peter Rosset, and Luis Esparza	*World Hunger: Twelve Myths.* New York: Grove Press, 1998.
Thomas A. Lyson	*Civic Agriculture: Reconnecting Farm, Food, and Community.* Boston: Tufts University Press, 2004.
Terry Marsden	*The New Regulation and Governance of Food: Beyond the Food Crisis?* London: Routledge, 2009.

Henry I. Miller and Gregory Conko	*The Frankenfood Myth: How Protest and Politics Threaten the Biotech Revolution.* Westport, CT: Praeger Publishers, 2004.
Raj Patel	*Stuffed and Starved: The Hidden Battle for the World Food System.* New York: Melville House, 2008.
Dale Allen Pfeiffer	*Eating Fossil Fuels: Oil, Food and the Coming Crisis in Agriculture.* Gabriola Island, British Columbia: New Society Publishers, 2006.
E.F. Schumacher	*Small is Beautiful: Economics as if People Mattered (25⁰ Anniversary Edition).* London: Hartley and Marks Publishers, 2000.
Vandana Shiva	*Stolen Harvest: The Hijacking of the Global Food Supply.* Cambridge: South End Press, 2000.
Vandana Shiva, ed.	*Manifestos on the Future of Food and Seed.* Cambridge: South End Press, 2007.
Peter Singer and Jim Mason	*The Ethics of What We Eat: Why Our Food Choices Matter.* Emmau, PA: Rodale Books, 2007.
Muhammad Yunus	*Creating a World Without Poverty: Social Business and the Future of Capitalism.* New York: PublicAffairs, 2009.

Periodicals

Anonymous	"The Silent Tsunami," *The Economist*, April 17, 2008.
Kaushik Basu	"How to Solve the Global Food Crisis," *BBCNews.com*, April 28, 2008.
Walden Bello	"Manufacturing a Food Crisis," *The Nation*, May 15, 2008.
Ben Crow	"The Unacknowledged Caused and Unprecedented Scale of the Global Food Crisis," *Third World Resurgence*, no. 212, April 2008.
Thalif Deen	"U.N. Seeks a Green Revolution in Food," *Inter-Press Service News*, February 19, 2009.
Jared Diamond	"What's Your Consumption Factor?" *The New York Times*, January 2, 2009.
J.R. Dunn	"The Food Crisis," *American Thinker*, April 29, 2008.
Karen Harper	"The Global Food Crisis: How the Market Has Driven Up Prices and Hunger," *Indybay.org*, June 12, 2008.
Simon Johnson	"Food and Biofuels: The Price of Success," *IMFSurvey Magazine*, December 3, 2007.
Mira Kamdar	"On the Front Lines of the Global Food Crisis," *Slate.com*, August 4–8, 2008.

Frances Moore Lappe	"The Shortage Isn't Food, Its Democracy," *Sojourners Magazine*, vol. 37, no. 7, July 2008.
Geoffrey Lean	"Multinationals Make Billions in Profit Out of Growing Global Food Crisis," *Independent*, May 4, 2008.
Ban Ki Moon and Rodriguez Zapatero	"Our Forgotten Crisis," *International Herald Tribune*, January 25, 2009.
John Nichols	"The World Food Crisis," *The Nation*, April 24, 2008.
Carl Pope	"The Real Villain in the World Food Crisis," *The Huffington Post*, May 19, 2008.
Nomi Prins	"Who Benefits from High Food Prices?" *Mother Jones*, June 19, 2008.
Jeffrey Sachs	"Surging Food Prices Mean Global Instability," *Scientific American*, May 19, 2008.
Jeffrey Sachs	"How to Solve the Growing Global Food Crisis, in Three Steps," *New York Daily News*, July 23, 2008.
Amartya Sen	"The Rich Get Hungrier," *The New York Times*, May 28, 2009.
Peter Singer	"Food Crisis Solution: Go Vegan," *Marketplace, NPR*, June 17, 2008.
Vivienne Walt	"The World's Growing Food-Price Crisis," *Time*, Feb. 27, 2008.

Index